Augustus Le Plongeon

Vestiges of the Mayas

Or, Facts Tending to Prove that Communications and Intimate Relations...

Augustus Le Plongeon

Vestiges of the Mayas
Or, Facts Tending to Prove that Communications and Intimate Relations...

ISBN/EAN: 9783744751711

Printed in Europe, USA, Canada, Australia, Japan

Cover: Foto ©ninafisch / pixelio.de

More available books at **www.hansebooks.com**

VESTIGES OF THE MAYAS,

OR,

Facts tending to prove that Communications and Intimate Relations must have existed, in very remote times, between the inhabitants of

MAYAB

AND THOSE OF

ASIA AND AFRICA.

BY

AUGUSTUS LE PLONGEON, M. D.,

Member of the American Antiquarian Society of Worcester, Mass., of the California Academy of Sciences, and several other Scientific Societies. Author of various Essays and Scientific Works.

NEW YORK:
JOHN POLHEMUS, PRINTER AND STATIONER,
102 NASSAU STREET.
1881.

TO

MR. PIERRE LORILLARD.

Who deserves the thanks of the students of American Archæology more than you, for the interest manifested in the explorations of the ruined monuments of Central America, handiwork of the races that inhabited this continent in remote ages, and the material help given by you to Foreign and American explorers in that field of investigations?

Accept, then, my personal thanks, with the dedication of this small Essay. It forms part of the result of many years' study and hardships among the ruined cities of the Incas, in Peru, and of the Mayas in Yucatan.

Yours very respectfully,

AUGUSTUS Le PLONGEON, M. D.

New York, *December* 15, 1881.

VESTIGES OF THE MAYAS.

YUCATAN is the peninsula which divides the Gulf of Mexico from the Caribbean Sea. It is comprised between the 17° 30′ and 21° 50′, of latitude north, and the 88° and 91° of longitude west from the Greenwich meridian.

The whole peninsula is of fossiferous limestone formation. Elevated a few feet only above the sea, on the coasts, it gradually raises toward the interior, to a maximum height of above 70 feet. A bird's-eye view, from a lofty building, impresses the beholder with the idea that he is looking on an immense sea of verdure, having the horizon for boundary; without a hill, not even a hillock, to break the monotony of the landscape. Here and there clusters of palm trees, or artificial mounds, covered with shrubs, loom above the green dead-level as islets, over that expanse of green foliage, affording a momentary relief to the eyes growing tired of so much sameness.

About fifty miles from the northwestern coast begins a low, narrow range of hills, whose highest point is not much above 500 feet. It traverses the peninsula in a direction a little south from east, commencing a few miles north from the ruined city of Uxmal, and terminating some distance from the eastern coast, opposite to the magnificent bay of Ascension.

Lately I have noticed that some veins of red oxide of iron exist among these hills—quarries of marble must also be found there; since the sculptured ornaments that adorn the facade of all the monuments at Uxmal are of that stone. To-day the inhabitants of Yucatan are even ignorant of the existence of these minerals in their country, and ocher to paint, and marble slabs to floor their houses, are imported from abroad. I have also discovered veins of good lithographic stones that could be worked at comparatively little expense.

The surface of the country is undulating; its stony waves recall forcibly to the mind the heavy swell of mid-ocean. It seems as if, in times long gone by, the soil was upheaved, *en masse*, from the bottom of the sea, by volcanic forces. This upheaval must have taken place many centuries ago, since isolated columns of *Katuns* 1m. 50c. square, erected at least 6,000 years ago, stand yet in the same perpendicular position, as at the time when another stone was added to those already piled up, to indicate a lapse of twenty years in the life of the nation.

It is, indeed, a remarkable fact, that whilst the surrounding countries—Mexico, Guatemala, Cuba and the other West India Islands—are frequently convulsed by earthquakes, the peninsula of Yucatan is entirely free from these awe-inspiring convulsions of mother earth. This immunity may be attributed, in my opinion, to the innumerable and extensive caves with which the whole country is entirely honeycombed; and the large number of immense natural wells, called Senotes, that are to be found everywhere. These caves and senotes afford an outlet for the escape of the gases generated in the superficial strata of the earth. These, finding no resistance to their passage, follow, harmlessly, these vents without producing on the surface any of those terrible commotions that fill the heart of man and beast alike with fright and dismay.

Some of those caves are said to be very extensive— None, however, has been thoroughly explored. I have visited a few, certainly extremely beautiful, adorned as they are with brilliant stalactites depending from their roofs, that seem as if supported by the stalagmites that must have required ages to be formed gradually from the floor into the massive columns, as we see them to-day.

In all the caves are to be found either inexhaustible

springs of clear, pure, cold water, or streams inhabited by shrimps and fishes. No one can tell whence they come or where they go. All currents of water are subterraneous. Not a river is to be found on the surface; not even the smallest of streamlets, where the birds of the air, or the wild beasts of the forests, can allay their thirst during the dry season. The plants, if there are no chinks or crevices in the stony soil through which their roots can penetrate and seek the life-sustaining fluid below, wither and die. It is a curious sight that presented by the roots of the trees, growing on the precipituous brinks of the *senotes*, in their search for water. They go down and down, even a hundred feet, until they reach the liquid surface, from where they suck up the fluid to aliment the body of the tree. They seem like many cables and ropes stretched all round the sides of the well; and, in fact, serves as such to some of the most daring of the natives, to ascend or descend to enjoy a refreshing bath.

These *senotes* are immense circular holes, the diameter of which varies from 50 to 500 feet, with perpendicular walls from 50 to 150 feet deep. These holes might be supposed to have served as ducts for the subterranean gases at the time of the upheaval of the country. Now they generally contain water. In some, the current is easily noticeable; many are completely dry; whilst others contain thermal mineral water, emitting at times strong sulphurous odor and vapor.

Many strange stories are told by the aborigines concerning the properties possessed by the water in certain senotes, and the strange phenomena that takes place in others. In one, for example, you are warned to approach the water walking backward, and to breathe very softly, otherwise it becomes turbid and unfit for drinking until it has settled and become clear again. In another you are told not to speak above a whisper, for if any one raises the voice the tranquil surface of the water immediately becomes agitated, and soon assumes the appearance of boiling; even its level raises. These and many other things are told in connection with the caves and senotes; and we find them mentioned in the writings of the chroniclers and historians from the time of the Spanish conquest.

No lakes exist on the surface, at least within the territories occupied by the white men. Some small sheets of water, called aguadas, may be found here and there, and are fed by the underground current; but they are very rare. There are three or four near the ruins of the ancient city of Mayapan : probably its inhabitants found in them an abundant supply of water. Following all the same direction, they are, as some suppose, no doubt with reason, the outbreaks of a subterranean stream that comes also to the surface in the senote of *Mucuyché*. A mile or so from Uxmal is another aguada ; but judging from the great number of artificial reservoirs, built on the terraces and in the courts of all the monuments, it would seem as if the people there depended more on the clouds for their provision of water than on the wells and senotes. Yet I feel confident that one of these must exist under the building known as the Governor's house; having discovered in its immediate vicinity the entrance—now closed—of a cave from which a cool current of air is continually issuing ; at times with great force.

I have been assured by Indians from the village of Chemax, who pretend to know that part of the country well, that, at a distance of about fifty miles from the city of Valladolid, the actual largest settlement on the eastern frontier, in the territories occupied by the SANTA CRUZ Indians, there exists, near the ruins of *Kaba*, two extensive sheets of water, from where, in years gone by, the inhabitants of Valladolid procured abundant supply of excellent fishes. These ruins of Kaba, said to be very interesting, have never been visited by any foreigner ; nor are they likely to be for many years to come, on account of the imminent danger of falling into the hands of those of Santa Cruz—that, since 1847, wage war to the knife against the Yucatecans.

On the coast, the sea penetrating in the lowlands have formed sloughs and lakes, on the shores of which thickets of mangroves grow, with tropical luxuriancy. Intermingling their crooked roots, they form such a barrier as to make landing well nigh impossible. These small lakes, subject to the ebb and flow of the tides, are the resort of innumerable sea birds and water fowls of all sizes and descriptions; from the snipe to the crane, and brightly colored flamingos, from the screeching sea gulls to the serious looking pelican. They are attracted to these lakes by the solitude of the forests of mangroves that afford them excellent shelter, where to build their nests, and find protection from the storms that, at certain season of the year, sweep with untold violence along the coast: and because with ease they can procure an abundant supply of food, these waters being inhabited by myriads of fishes, as they come to bask on the surface which is seldom ruffled even when the tempest rages outside.

Notwithstanding the want of superficial water, the air is always charged with moisture; the consequence being a most equable temperature all the year round, and an extreme luxuriance of all vegetation. The climate is mild and comparatively healthy for a country situated within the tropics, and bathed by the waters of the Mexican Gulf. This mildness and healthiness may be attributed to the sea breezes that constantly pass over the peninsula, carrying the malaria and noxious gases that have not been absorbed by the forests, which cover the main portion of the land; and to the great abundance of oxygen exuded by the plants in return. This excessive moisture and the decomposition of dead vegetable matter is the cause of the intermittent fevers that prevail in all parts of the peninsula, where the yellow fever, under a mild form generally, is also endemic. When it appears, as this year, in an epidemic form, the natives themselves enjoy no immunity from its ravages, and fall victims to it as well as unacclimated foreigners.

These epidemics, those of smallpox and other diseases that at times make their appearance in Yucatan, generally present themselves after the rainy season, particularly if the rains have been excessive. The country being extremely flat, the drainage is necessarily very bad : and in places like Merida, for example, where a crowding of population exists, and the cleanliness of the streets is utterly disregarded by the proper authorities, the decomposition of vegetable and animal matter is very large; and the miasmas generated, being carried with the vapors arising from the constant evaporation of stagnant waters, are the origin of those scourges that decimate the inhabitants. Yucatan, isolated as it is, its small territory nearly surrounded by water, ought to be, if the laws of health were properly enforced, one of the most healthy countries on the earth; where, as in the Island of Cozumel, people should only die of old age or accident. The thermometer varies but little, averaging about 80° *Far*. True, it rises in the months of July and August as high as 96° in the shade, but it seldom falls below 65° in the month of December. In the dry season, from January to June, the trees become divested of their leaves, that fall more particularly in March and April. Then the sun, returning from the south on its way to the north, passes over the land and darts its scorching perpendicular rays on it, causing every living creature to thirst for a drop of cool water; the heat being increased by the burning of those parts of the forests that have been cut down to prepare fields for cultivation.

In the portion of the peninsula, about one-third of it, that still remains in possession of the white, the Santa Cruz Indians holding, since 1847, the richest and most fertile, two-thirds, the soil is entirely stony. The arable loam, a few inches in thickness, is the result of the detriti of the stones, mixed with the remainder of the decomposition of vegetable matter. In certain districts, towards the eastern and southern parts of the State, patches of red clay form excellent ground for the cultivation of the sugar cane and Yuca root. From this an excellent starch is obtained in large quantities. Withal, the soil is of astonishing fertility, and trees, even, are met with of large size, whose roots run on the surface of the bare stone, penetrating the chinks and crevices only in search of moisture. Often times I have seen them growing from the center of slabs, the seed having fallen in a hole that happened to be bored in them. In the month of May the whole country seems parched and dry. Not a leaf, not a bud. The branches and boughs are naked and covered with a thick coating of gray dust. Nothing to intercept the sight in the thicket but the bare trunks and branches, with the withes entwining them. With the first days of June come the first refreshing showers. As if a magic wand had been waved over the land, the view changes—life springs everywhere. In the short space of a few days the forests have resumed their holiday attire ; buds appear and the leaves shoot ; the flowers bloom sending forth their fragrance, that wafted by the breeze perfume the air far and near. The birds sing their best songs of joy ; the insects chirp their shrillest notes ; butterflies of gorgeous colors flutter in clouds in every direction in search of the nectar contained in the cups of the newly-opened blossom, and dispute it with the brilliant humming-birds. All creation rejoices because a few tears of mother Nature have brought joy and happiness to all living beings, from the smallest blade of grass to the majestic palm ; from the creeping worm to man, who proudly titles himself the lord of creation.

Yucatan has no rich metallic mines, but its wealth of vegetable productions is immense. Large forests of mahogany, cedar, zapotillo trees cover vast extents of land in the eastern and southern portions of the peninsula; whilst patches of logwood and mora, many miles in length, grow near the coast. The wood is to-day cut down and exported by the Indians of Santa Cruz through their agents at Belize. Coffee, vanilla, tobacco, india-rubber, rosins of various kinds, copal in particular, all of good quality, abound in the country, but are not cultivated on account of its unsettled state; the Indians retaining possession of the most fertile territories where these rich products are found.

The whites have been reduced to the culture of the Hennequen plant (agave sisalensis) in order to subsist. It is the only article of commerce that grows well on the stony soil to which they are now confined. The filament obtained from the plant, and the objects manufactured from it constitute the principal article of export; in fact the only source of wealth of the Yucatecans. As the filament is now much in demand for the fabrication of cordage in the United States and Europe, many of the landowners have ceased to plant maize, although the staple article of food in all classes, to convert their land into hennequen fields. The plant thrives well on stony soil, requires no water and but little care. The natural consequence of planting the whole country with hennequen has been so great a deficiency in the maize crop, that this year not enough was grown for the consumption, and people in the northeastern district were beginning to suffer from the want of it, when some merchants of Merida imported large quantities from New York. They, of course, sold it at advanced prices, much to the detriment of the poorer classes. Some sugar is also cultivated in the southern and eastern districts, but not in sufficient quantities even for the consumption; and not a little is imported from Habana.

The population of the country, about 250,000 souls all told, are mostly Indians and mixed blood. In fact, very few families can be found of pure Caucasian race. Notwithstanding the great admixture of different races, a careful observer can readily distinguish yet four prominent ones, very noticeable by their features, their stature, the conformation of their body. The dwarfish race is certainly easily distinguishable from the descendants of the giants that tradition says once upon a time existed in the country, whose bones are yet found, and whose portraits are painted on the walls of Chaacmol's funeral chamber at Chichen-Itza. The almond-eyed, flat-nosed Siamese race of Copan is not to be mistaken for the long, big-nosed, flat-headed remnant of the Nahualt from Palenque, who are said to have invaded the country some time at the beginning of the Christian era; and whose advent among the Mayas, whose civilization they appear to have destroyed, has been commemorated by calling the *west*, the region whence they came, according to Landa, Cogolludo and other historians, NOHNIAL, a word which means literally *big noses for our daughters;* whilst the coming of the bearded men from the *east*, better looking than those of the west, if we are to give credit to the bas-relief where their portraits are to be seen, was called CENIAL—*ornaments for our daughters.*

If we are to judge by the great number of ruined cities scattered everywhere through the forests of the peninsula; by the architectural beauty of the monuments still extant, the specimens of their artistic attainments in drawing and sculpture which have reached us in the bas-reliefs, statues and mural paintings of Uxmal and Chichen-Itza; by their knowledge in mathematical and astronomical sciences, as manifested in the construction of the gnomon found by me in the ruins of Mayapan; by the complexity of the grammatical form and syntaxis of their language, still spoken to-day by the majority of the inhabitants of Yucatan; by their mode of expressing their thoughts on paper, made from the bark of certain trees, with alphabetical and phonetical characters, we must of necessity believe that, at some time or other, the country was not only densely populated, but that the inhabitants had reached a high degree of civilization. To-day we can conceive of very few of their attainments by the scanty remains of their handiwork, as they have come to us injured by the hand of time, and, more so yet, by that of man, during the wars, the invasions, the social and religious convulsions which have taken place among these people, as among all other nations. Only the opening of the buildings which contain the libraries of their learned men, and the reading of their works, could solve the mystery, and cause us to know how much they had advanced in the discovery and explanation of Nature's arcana; how much they knew of mankind's past history, and of the nations with which they held intercourse. Let us hope that the day may yet come when the Mexican government will grant to me the requisite permission, in order that I may bring forth, from the edifices where they are hidden, the precious volumes, without opposition from the owners of the property where the monuments exist. Until then we must content ourselves with the study of the inscriptions carved on the walls, and becoming acquainted with the history of their builders, and continue to conjecture what knowledge they possessed in order to be able to rear such enduring structures, besides the art of designing the plans and ornaments, and the manner of carving them on stone.

Let us place ourselves in the position of the archæologists of thousands of years to come, examining the ruins of our great cities, finding still on foot some of the stronger built palaces and public buildings, with some rare specimens of the arts, sciences, industry of our days, the minor edifices having disappeared, gnawed by the steely tooth of time, together with the many products of our industry, the machines of all kinds, creation of man's ingenuity, and his powerful helpmates. What would they know of the attainments and the progress in mechanics of our days? Would they be able to form a complete idea of our civilization, and of the knowledge of our scientific men, without the help of the volumes contained in our public libraries, and maybe of some one able to interpret them? Well, it seems to me that we stand in exactly the same position concerning the civilization of those who have preceded us five or ten thousand years ago on this continent, as these future archæologists may stand regarding our civilization five or ten thousand years hence.

It is a fact, recorded by all historians of the Conquest, that when for the first time in 1517 the Spaniards came in sight of the lands called by them Yucatan, they were surprised to see on the coast many monuments well built of stone; and to find the country strewn with large cities and beautiful monuments that recalled to their memory the best of Spain. They were no less astonished to meet in the inhabitants, not naked savages, but a civilized people, possessed of polite and pleasant manners, dressed in white cotton habiliments, navigating large boats propelled by sails, traveling on well constructed roads and causeways that, in point of beauty and solidity, could compare advantageously with similar Roman structures in Spain, Italy, England or France.

I will not describe here the majestic monuments raised by the Mayas. Mrs. Le Plongeon, in her letters to the *New York World*, has given of those of UXMAL, AKE and MAYAPAN, the only correct description ever published. My object at present is to relate some of the curious facts revealed to us by their weather-beaten and crumbling walls, and show how erroneous is the opinion of some European scientists, who think it not worth while to give a moment of their precious time to the study of American archæology, because say they: *No relations have ever been found to have existed between the monuments and civilizations of the inhabitants of this continent and those of the old world.* On what ground they hazard such an opinion it is difficult to surmise, since to my knowledge the ancient ruined cities of Yucatan, until lately, have never been thoroughly, much less scientifically, explored. The same is true of the other monumental ruins of the whole of Central America.

When Mrs. Le Plongeon and myself landed at Progresso, in 1873, we thought that because we had read the works of Stephens, Waldeck, Norman, Fredeichstal; carefully examined the few photographic views made by Mr. Charnay of some of the monuments, we knew all about them. Alas! vain presumption! When in presence of the antique shrines and palaces of the Mayas, we soon saw how mistaken we had been; how little those writers had seen of the monuments they had pretended to describe: that the work of studying them systematically was not even begun; and that many years of close observation and patient labor would be necessary in order to dispel the mysteries which hang over them, and to discover the hidden meaning of their ornaments and inscriptions. To this difficult task we resolved to dedicate our time, and to concentrate our efforts to find a solution, if possible, to the enigma.

We began our work by taking photographs of all the monuments in their *tout ensemble*, and in all their details, as much as practicable. Next, we surveyed them carefully; made accurate plans of them in order to be able to comprehend by the disposition of their different parts, for what possible use they were erected; taking, as a starting point, that the human mind and human inclinations and wants are the same in all times, in all countries, in all races when civilized and cultured. We next carefully examined what connection the ornaments bore to each other, and tried to understand the meaning of the designs. At first the maze of these designs seemed a very difficult riddle to solve. Yet, we believed that if a human intelligence had devised it, another human intelligence would certainly be able to unravel it. It was not, however, until we had nearly completed the tracing and study of the mural paintings, still extant in the funeral chamber of Chaacmol, or room built on the top of the eastern wall of the gymnasium at Chichen-Itza, at its southern end, that Stephens mistook for a shrine dedicated to the god of the players at ball, that a glimmer of light began to dawn upon us. In tracing the figure of Chaacmol in battle, I remarked that the shield worn by him had painted on it round green spots, and was exactly like the ornaments placed between tiger and tiger on the entablature of the same monument. I naturally concluded that the monument had been raised to the memory of the warrior bearing the shield; that the tigers represented his totem, and that *Chaacmol* or *Balam* maya words for spotted tiger or leopard, was his name. I then remembered that at about one hundred yards in the thicket from the edifice, in an easterly direction, a few days before, I had noticed the ruins of a remarkable mound of rather small dimensions. It was ornamented with slabs engraved with the images of spotted tigers, eating human hearts, forming magnificent bas-reliefs, conserving yet traces of the colors in which it was formerly painted. I repaired to the place. Doubts were no longer possible. The same round dots, forming the spots of their skins, were present here as on the shield of the warrior in battle, and that on the entablature of the building. On examining carefully the ground around the mound, I soon stumbled upon what seemed to be a half buried statue. On clearing the *débris* we found a statue in the round, representing a wounded tiger reclining on his right side. Three holes in the back indicated the places where he received his wounds. It was headless. A few feet further, I found a human head with the eyes half closed, as those of a dying person. When placed on the neck of the tiger it fitted exactly. I propped it with sticks to keep it in place. So arranged, it recalled vividly the Chaldean and Egyptian deities having heads of human beings and bodies of animals. The next object that called my attention was another slab on which was represented in bas-relief a dying warrior, reclining on his back, the head was thrown entirely backwards. His left arm was placed across his chest, the left hand resting on the right shoulder, exactly in the same position which the Egyptians were wont, at times, to give to the mummies of some of their eminent men. From his mouth was seen escaping two thin, narrow flames—the spirit of the dying man abandoning the body with the last warm breath.

These and many other sculptures caused me to suspect that this monument had been the mausoleum raised to the memory of the warrior with the shield covered with the round dots. Next to the slabs engraved with the image of tigers was another, representing an *ara militaris* (a bird of the parrot specie, very large and of brilliant plumage of various colors). I took it for the totem of his wife, MOÓ, *macaw;* and so it proved to be when later I was able to interpret their ideographic writings. *Kinich-Kakmó* after her death obtained the honors of the apotheosis ; had temples raised to her memory, and was worshipped at Izamal up to the time of the Spanish conquest, according to Landa, Cogolludo and Lizana.

Satisfied that I had found the tomb of a great warrior among the Mayas, I resolved to make an excavation, notwithstanding I had no tools or implements proper for such work. After two months of hard toil, after penetrating through three level floors painted with yellow ochre, at last a large stone urn came in sight. It was opened in presence of Colonel D. Daniel Traconis. It contained a small heap of grayish dust over which lay the cover of a terra cotta pot, also painted yellow ; a few small ornaments of macre that crumbled to dust on being touched, and a large ball of jade, with a hole pierced in the middle. This ball had at one time been highly polished, but for some cause or other the polish had disappeared from one side. Near, and lower than the urn, was discovered the head of the colossal statue, to-day the best, or one of the best pieces, in the National Museum of Mexico, having been carried thither on board of the gunboat *Libertad*, without my consent, and without any renumeration having even been offered by the Mexican government for my labor, my time and the money spent in the discovery. Close to the chest of the statue was another stone urn much larger than the first. On being uncovered it was found to contain a large quantity of reddish substance and some jade ornaments. On closely examining this substance I pronounced it organic matter that had been subjected to a very great heat in an open vessel. (A chemical anylysis of some of it by Professor Thompson, of Worcester, Mass., at the request of Mr. Stephen Salisbury, Jr., confirmed my opinion). From the position of the urn I made up my mind that its contents were the heart and viscera of the personage represented by the statue; while the dust found in the first urn must have been the residue of his brains.

Landa tells us that it was the custom, even at the time of the Spanish conquest, when a person of eminence died to make images of stone, or terra cotta or wood in the semblance of the deceased, whose ashes were placed in a hollow made on the back of the head for the purpose. Feeling sorry for having thus disturbed the remains of *Chaacmol*, so carefully concealed by his friends and relatives many centuries ago; in order to save them from further desecration, I burned the greater part reserving only a small quantity for future analysis. This finding of the heart and brains of that chieftain, afforded an explanation, if any was needed, of one of the scenes more artistically portrayed in the mural paintings of his funeral chamber. In this scene which is painted immediately over the entrance of the chamber, where is also a life-size representation of his corpse prepared for cremation, the dead warrior is pictured stretched on the ground, his back resting on a large stone placed for the purpose of raising the body and keeping open the cut made across it, under the ribs, for the extraction of the heart and other parts it was customary to preserve. These are seen in the hands of his children. At the feet of the statue were found a number of beautiful arrowheads of flint and chalcedony; also beads that formed part of his necklace. These, to-day petrified, seemed to have been originally of bone or ivory. They were wrought to figure shells of periwinkles. Surrounding the slab on which the figure rests was a large quantity of dried blood. This fact might lead us to suppose that slaves were sacrificed at his funeral, as Herodotus tells us it was customary with the Scythians, and we know it was with the Romans and other nations of the old world, and the Incas in Peru. Yet not a bone or any other human remains were found in the mausoleum.

The statue forms a single piece with the slab on which it reclines, as if about to rise on his elbows, the legs being drawn up so that the feet rest flat on the slab. I consider this attitude given to the statues of dead personages that I have discovered in Chichen, where they are still, to be symbolical of their belief in reincarnation. They, in common with the Egyptians, the Hindoos, and other nations of antiquity, held that the spirit of man after being made to suffer for its shortcomings during its mundane life, would enjoy happiness for a time proportionate to its good deeds, then return to earth, animate the body and live again a material existence. The Mayas, however, destroying the body by fire, made statues in the semblance of the deceased, so that, being indestructible the spirit might find and animate them on its return to earth. The present aborigines have the same belief. Even to-day, they never fail to prepare the *hanal pixan*, the food for the spirits, which they place in secluded spots in the forests or fields, every year, in the month of November. These statues also hold an urn between their hands. This fact again recalls to the mind the Egpptian custom of placing an urn in the coffins with the mummies, to indicate that the spirit of the deceased had been judged and found righteous.

The ornament hanging on the breast of Chaacmol's effigy, from a ribbon tied with a peculiar knot behind his neck, is simply a badge of his rank; the same is seen on the breast of many other personages in the bas-reliefs and mural paintings. A similar mark of authority is yet in usage in Burmah.

I have tarried so long on the description of my first important discovery because I desired to explain the method followed by me in the investigation of these monuments, to show that the result of our labors are by no means the work of imagination—as some have been so kind a *short* time ago as to intimate—but of careful and patient analysis and comparison ; also, in order, from the start, to call your attention to the similarity of certain customs in the funeral rites that the Mayas seem to have possessed in common with other nations of the old world : and lastly, because my friend, Dr. Jesus Sanchez, Professor of Archæology in the National Museum of Mexico, ignoring altogether the circumstances accompanying the discovery of the statue, has published in the *Anales del Museo Nacional,* a long dissertation—full of erudition, certainly— to prove that the statue discovered by me at Chichen-Itza, was a representation of the *God of the natural production of the earth,* and that the name given by me was altogether arbitrary; and , also, because an article has appeared in the *North American Review* for October, 1880, signed by Mr. Charnay, in which the author, after re-producing Mr. Sanchez's writing, pronounces *ex cathedra* and *de perse,* but without assigning any reason for his opinion, that the statue is the effigy of the *god of wine*—the Mexican Bacchus—without telling us which of them, for there were two.

Having been obliged to abandon the statue in the forests—well wrapped in oilcloth, and sheltered under a hut of palm leaves, constructed by Mrs. Le Plongeon and myself—my men having been disarmed by order of General Palomino, then commander-in-chief of the federal forces in Yucatan, in consequence of a revolutionary movement against Dr. Sebastian Lerdo de Tejada and in favor of General Diaz—I went to Uxmal to continue my researches among its ruined temples and palaces. There I took many photographs, surveyed the monuments, and, for the first time, found the remnants of the phallic worship of the Nahualts. Its symbols are not to be seen in Chichen—the city of the holy and learned men, Itzaes—but are frequently met with in the northern parts of the peninsula, and all the regions where the Nahualt influence predominated.

There can be no doubt that in very ancient times the same customs and religious worship existed in Uxmal and Chichen, since these two cities were founded by the same family, that of CAN (serpent), whose name is written on all the monuments in both places. CAN and the members of his family worshipped Deity under the symbol of the mastodon's head. At Chichen a tableau of said worship forms the ornament of the building, designated in the work of Stephens, "Travels in Yucatan," as IGLESIA ; being, in fact, the north wing of the palace and museum. This is the reason why the mastodon's head forms so prominent a feature in all the ornaments of the edifices built by them. They also worshipped the sun and fire, which they represented by the same hieroglyph used by the Egyptians for the sun ☉. In this worship of the fire they resembled the Chaldeans and Hindoos, but differed from the Egyptians, who had no veneration for this element. They regarded it merely as an animal that devoured all things within its reach, and died with all it had swallowed, when replete and satisfied.

From certain inscriptions and pictures—in which the *Cans* are represented crawling on all fours like dogs—sculptured on the façade of their house of worship, it would appear that their religion of the mastodon was replaced by that of the reciprocal forces of nature, imported in the country by the big-nosed invaders, the Nahualts coming from the west. These destroyed Chichen, and established their capital at *Uxmal*. There they erected in all the courts of the palaces, and on the platforms of the temples the symbols of their religion, taking care, however, not to interfere with the worship of the sun and fire, that seems to have been the most popular.

Bancroft in his work, "*The Native Races of the Pacific States*," Vol. IV., page 277, remarks : "That the " scarcity of idols among the Maya antiquities must be

" regarded as extraordinary. That the people of Yuca-
" tan were idolators there is no possible doubt, and in
" connection with the magnificent shrines and temples
" erected by them, and rivalling or excelling the grand
" obelisks of Copan, might naturally be sought for, but
" in view of the facts it must be concluded that the
" Maya idols were very small, and that such as escaped
" the fatal iconoclasms of the Spanish ecclesiastics were
" buried by the natives as the only means of preventing
" their desecration."

That the people who inhabited the country at the time of the Spanish conquest had a multiplicity of gods there can be no doubt. The primitive form of worship, with time and by the effect of invasions from outside, had disappeared, and been replaced by that of their great men and women, who were deified and had temples raised to their memory, as we see, for example, in the case of *Moo*, wife and sister of Chaacmol, whose shrine was built on the high mound on the north side of the large square in the city of Izamal. There pilgrims flocked from all parts of the country to listen to the oracles delivered by the mouth of her priests; and see the goddess come down from the clouds every day, at mid-day, under the form of a resplendent macaw, and light the fire that was to consume the offerings deposited on her altar; even at the time of the conquest, according to the chroniclers, Chaacmol himself seems to have become the god of war, that always appeared in the midst of the battle, fighting on the side of his followers, surrounded with flames. Kukulcan, "the culture" hero of the Mayas, the winged serpent, worshipped by the Mexicans as the god Guetzalcoalt, and by the Quichés as Cucumatz, if not the father himself of Chaacmol, CAN, at least one of his ancestors.

The friends and followers of that prince may have worshipped him after his death, and the following generations, seeing the representation of his totems (serpent) covered with feathers, on the walls of his palaces, and of the sanctuaries built by him to the deity, called him·

Kukulcan, the winged serpent: when, in fact, the artists who carved his emblems on the walls covered them with the cloaks he and all the men in authority and the high priests wore on ceremonial occasions—feathered vestments—as we learned from the study of mural paintings.

In the temples and palaces of the ancient Mayas I have never seen anything that I could in truth take for idols. I have seen many symbols, such as double-headed tigers, corresponding to the double-headed lions of the Egyptians, emblems of the sun. I have seen the representation of people kneeling in a peculiar manner, with their right hand resting on the left shoulder—sign of respect among the Mayas as among the inhabitants of Egypt—in the act of worshiping the mastodon head; but I doubt if this can be said to be idol worship. *Can* and his family were probably monotheists. The masses of the people, however, may have placed the different natural phenomena under the direct supervision of special imaginary beings, prescribing to them the same duties that among the Catholics are prescribed, or rather attributed, to some of the saints; and may have tributed to them the sort of worship of *dulia*, tributed to the saints—even made images that they imagined to represent such or such deity, as they do to-day; but I have never found any. They worshiped the divine essence, and called it Kú.

In course of time this worship may have been replaced by idolatrous rites, introduced by the barbarous or half civilized tribes which invaded the country, and implanted among the inhabitants their religious belief, their idolatrous superstitions and form of worship with their symbols. The monuments of Uxmal afford ample evidence of that fact.

My studies, however, have nothing to do with the history of the country posterior to the invasion of the Nahualts. These people appear to have destroyed the high form of civilization existing at the time of their advent; and tampered with the ornaments of the buildings in order to introduce the symbols of the reciprocal forces of nature.

The language of the ancient Mayas, strange as it may appear, has survived all the vicissitudes of time, wars, and political and religious convulsions. It has, of course, somewhat degenerated by the mingling of so many races in such a limited space as the peninsula of Yucatan is; but it is yet the vernacular of the people. The Spaniards themselves, who strived so hard to wipe out all vestiges of the ancient customs of the aborigines, were unable to destroy it; nay, they were obliged to learn it; and now many of their descendants have forgotten the mother tongue of their sires, and speak Maya only.

In some localities in Central America it is still spoken in its pristine purity, as, for example, by the *Chaacmules*, a tribe of bearded men, it is said, who live in the vicinity of the unexplored ruins of the ancient city of *Tekal*. It is a well-known fact that many tribes, as that of the Itzaes, retreating before the Nahualt invaders, after the surrender and destruction of their cities, sought refuge in the islands of the lake *Peten* of to-day, and called it *Peten-itza*, the *islands of the Itzaes;* or in the well nigh inaccessible valleys, defended by ranges of towering mountains. There they live to-day, preserving the customs, manners, language of their forefathers unaltered, in the tract of land known to us as *Tierra de Guerra*. No white man has ever penetrated their zealously guarded stronghold that lays between Guatemala, Tabasco, Chiapas and Yucatan, the river *Uzumasinta* watering part of their territory.

The Maya language seems to be one of the oldest tongues spoken by man, since it contains words and expressions of all, or nearly all, the known polished languages on earth. The name *Maya*, with the same signification everywhere it is met, is to be found scattered over the different countries of what we term the Old World, as in Central America.

I beg to call your attention to the following facts. They may have no significance. They may be mere coincidences, the strange freaks of hazard, of no possible value in the opinion of some among the learned men of our days. Just as the finding of English words and English customs, as now exist among the most remote nations and heterogeneous people and tribes of all races and colors, who do not even suspect the existence of one another, may be regarded by the learned philologists and ethonologists of two or three thousand years hence. These will, perhaps, also pretend that *these coincidences* are simply the curious workings of the human mind—the efforts of men endeavoring to express their thoughts in language, that being reduced to a certain number of sounds, must, of necessity produce, if not the same, at least very similar words to express the same idea—and that this similarity does not prove that those who invented them had, at any time, communication, unless, maybe, at the time of the building of the hypothetical Tower of Babel. Then all the inhabitants of earth are said to have bid each other a friendly good night, a certain evening, in a universal tongue, to find next morning that everybody had gone stark mad during the night: since each one, on meeting sixty-nine of his friends, was greeted by every one in a different and unknown manner, according to learned rabbins; and that he could no more understand what they said, than they what he said

It is very difficult without the help of the books of the learned priests of *Mayab* to know positively why they gave that name to the country known to-day as Yucatan. I can only surmise that they so called it from the great absorbant quality of its stony soil, which, in an incredibly short time, absorbs the water at the surface. This percolating through the pores of the stone is afterward found filtered clear and cool in the senotes and caves. *Mayab*, in the Maya language, means a tammy, a sieve. From the name of the country, no doubt, the Mayas took their name, as natural; and that name is found, as that of the English to-day, all over the ancient civilized world.

When, on January 28, 1873, I had the honor of reading a paper before the New York American Geographical Society—on the coincidences that exist between the monuments, customs, religious rites, etc. of the prehistoric inhabitants of America and those of Asia and Egypt—I pointed to the fact that sun circles, dolmen and tumuli, similar to the megalithic monuments of America, had been found to exist scattered through the islands of the Pacific to Hindostan; over the plains of the peninsulas at the south of Asia, through the deserts of Arabia, to the northern parts of Africa; and that not only these rough monuments of a primitive age, but those of a far more advanced civilization were also to be seen in these same countries. Allow me to repeat now what I then said regarding these strange facts: If we start from the American continent and travel towards the setting sun we may be able to trace the route followed by the mound builders to the plains of Asia and the valley of the Nile. The mounds scattered through the valley of the Mississippi seem to be the rude specimens of that kind of architecture. Then come the more highly finished teocalis of Yucatan and Mexico and Peru; the pyramidal mounds of *Maui*, one of the Sandwich Islands; those existing in the Fejee and other islands of the Pacific; which, in China, we find converted into the high, porcelain, gradated towers; and these again converted into the more imposing temples of Cochin-China, Hindostan, Ceylon—so grand, so stupendous in their wealth of ornamentation that those of Chichen-Itza Uxmal, Palenque, admirable as they are, well nigh dwindle into insignificance, as far as labor and imagination are concerned, when compared with them. That they present the same fundamental conception in their architecture is evident—a platform rising over another platform, the one above being of lesser size than the one below; the American monuments serving, as it were, as models for the more elaborate and perfect, showing the advance of art and knowledge.

The name Maya seems to have existed from the remotest times in the meridional parts of Hindostan. Valmiki, in his epic poem, the Ramayana, said to be written 1500 before the Christian era, in which he recounts the wars and prowesses of RAMA in the recovery of-his lost wife, the beautiful SITA, speaking of the country inhabited by the Mayas, describes it as abounding in mines of silver and gold, with precious stones and lapiz lazuri: and bounded by the *Vindhya* mountains on one side, the *Prastravana* range on the other and the sea on the third. The emissaries of RAMA having entered by mistake within the Mayas territories, learned that all foreigners were forbidden to penetrate into them; and that those who were so imprudent as to violate this prohibition, even through ignorance, seldom escaped being put to death. (Strange to say, the same thing happens to-day to those who try to penetrate into the territories of the *Santa Cruz* Indians, or in the valleys occupied by the *Lacandones, Itzaes* and other tribes that inhabit *La Tierra de Guerra*. The Yucatecans themselves do not like foreigners to go, and less to settle, in their country—are consequently opposed to immigration.

The emissaries of Rama, says the poet, met in the forest a woman who told them: That in very remote ages a prince of the Davanas, a learned magician, possessed of great power, whose name was *Maya*, established himself in the country, and that he was the architect of the principal of the Davanas: but having fallen in love with the nymph *Hemá*, married her; whereby he roused the jealousy of the god *Pourandura*, who attacked and killed him with a thunderbolt. Now, it is worthy of notice, that the word *Hem* signifies in the Maya language to *cross with ropes*; or according to Brasseur, *hidden mysteries*.

By a most rare coincidence we have the same identical story recorded in the mural paintings of Chaacmol's funeral chamber, and in the sculptures of Chichsen and Uxmal. There we find that Chaacmol, the husband of Moó is killed by his brother Aac, who stabbed him three times in the back with his spear for jealousy. Aac was in love with his sister Moó, but she married his brother Chaacmol from choice, and because the law of the country prescribed that the younger brother should marry his sister, making it a crime for the older brothers to marry her.

In another part of the *Ramayana*, MAYA is described as a powerful *Asoura*, always thirsting for battles and full of arrogance and pride—an enemy to Bāli, chief of one of the monkey tribes, by whom he was finally vanquished. The celebrated Indianist, Mr. H. T. Colebrooke, in a memoir on the sacred books of the Hindoos, published in Vol. VIII of the "Asiatic Researches," says: "The *Soûryasiddkântu* (the most ancient Indian treatise on astronomy), is not considered as written by MAYA; but this personage is represented as receiving his science from a partial incarnation of the sun."

MAYA is also, according to the Rig-Veda, the goddess, by whom all things are created by her union with Brahma. She is the cosmic egg, the golden uterus, the *Hiramyagarbha*. We see an image of it, represented floating amidst the water, in the sculptures that adorn the panel over the door of the east facade of the monument, called by me palace and museum at Chichen-Itza. Emile Burnouf, in his Sanscrit Dictionary, at the word Maya, says: Maya, an architect of the *Datyas*; Maya (*mas.*), magician, prestidigitator; (*fem.*) illusion, prestige; Maya, the magic virtue of the gods, their power for producing all things; also the feminine or producing energy of Brahma.

I will complete the list of these remarkable coincidences with a few others regarding customs exactly similar in both countries. One of these consists in carrying children astride on the hip in Yucatan as in India. In Yucatan this custom is accompanied by a very interesting ceremony called *hetzmec*. It is as follows: When a child reaches the age of four months an invitation is sent to the friends and members of the family of the parents to assemble at their house. Then in presence of all assembled the legs of the child are opened, and he is placed astride the hip of the *nailah* or *hetzmec* godmother; she in turn encircling the little one with her arm, supports him in that position whilst she walks five times round the house. During the time she is occupied in that walk five eggs are placed in hot ashes, so that they may burst and the five senses of the child be opened. By the manner in which they burst and the time they require for bursting, they pretend to know if he will be intelligent or not. During the ceremony they place in his tiny hands the implement pertaining to the industry he is expected to practice. The *nailah* is henceforth considered as a second mother to the child; who, when able to understand, is made to respect her: and she is expected, in case of the mother's death, to adopt and take care of the child as if he were her own.

Now, I will call your attention to another strange and most remarkable custom that was common to the inhabitants of *Mayab*, some tribes of the aborigines of North America, and several of those that dwell in Hindostan, and practice it even to-day. I refer to the printing of the human hand, dipped in a red colored liquid, on the walls of certain sacred edifices. Could not this custom, existing amongst nations so far apart, unknown to each other, and for apparently the same purposes, be considered as a link in the chain of evidence tending to prove that very intimate relations and communications have existed anciently between their ancestors? Might it not help the ethnologists to follow the migrations of the human race from this western continent to the eastern and southern shores of Asia, across the wastes of the Pacific Ocean? I am told by unimpeachable witnesses that they have seen the red or bloody hand in more than one of the temples of the South Sea islanders; and his Excellency Fred. P. Barlee, Esq., the actual governor of British Honduras, has assured me that he has examined this seemingly indelible imprint of the red hand on some rocks in caves in Australia. There is scarcely a monument in Yucatan that does not preserve the imprint of the open upraised hand, dipped in red paint of some sort, perfectly visible on its walls. I lately took tracings of two of these imprints that exist in the back saloon of the main hall, in the governor's house at Uxmal, in order to calculate the height of the personage who thus attested to those of his race, as I learned from one of my Indian friends, who passes for a wizard, that the building was *in naá*, my house. I may well say that the archway of the palace of the priests, toward the court, was nearly covered with them. Yet I am not aware that such symbol was ever used by the inhabitants of the countries bordering on the shores of the Mediterranean or by the Assyrians, or that it ever was discovered among the ruined temples or palaces of Egypt.

The meaning of the red hand used by the aborigines of some parts of America has been, it is well known, a subject of discussion for learned men and scientific societies. Its uses as a symbol remained for a long time a matter of conjecture. It seems that Mr. Schoolcraft had truly arrived at the knowledge of its veritable meaning. Effectively, in the 2d column of the 5th page of the *New York Herald* for April 12, 1879, in the account of the visit paid by Gen. Grant to Ram Singh, Maharajah of Jeypoor, we read the description of an excursion to the town of Amber. Speaking of the journey to the *home of an Indian king,* among other things the writer says :—
"We passed small temples, some of them ruined, some
"others with offerings of grains, or fruits, or flowers,
"some with priests and people at worship. On the walls
"of some of the temples we saw the marks of the human
"hand as though it had been steeped in blood and pres-
"sed against the white wall. We were told that it was
"the custom, when seeking from the gods some benison
"to note the vow by putting the hand into a liquid and
"printing it on the wall. This was to remind the gods
"of the vow and prayer. And if it came to pass in the
"shape of rain, or food, or health, or children, the joy-

"ous devotee returned to the temple and made other "offerings." In Yucatan it seems to have had the same meaning. That is to say: that the owners of the house if private, or the priests, in the temples and public buildings, called upon the edifices at the time of taking possession and using them for the first time, the blessing of the Deity; and placed the hand's imprints on the walls to recall the vows and prayer: and also, as the interpretation communicated to me by the Indians seems to suggest, as a signet or mark of property—*in naá*, my house.

I need not speak of the similarity of many religious rites and beliefs existing in Hindostan and among the inhabitants of *Mayab*. The worship of the fire, of the phallus, of Deity under the symbol of the mastodon's head, recalling that of Ganeza, the god with an elephant's head, hence that of the elephant in Siam, Birmah and other places of the Asiatic peninsula even in our day; and various other coincidences so numerous and remarkable that many would not regard them as simple coincidences. What to think, effectively, of the types of the personages whose portraits are carved on the obelisks of Copan? Were they in Siam instead of Honduras, who would doubt but they are Siameeses. What to say of the figures of men and women sculptured on the walls of the stupendous temples hewn, from the live rock, at Elephanta, so American is their appearance and features? Who would not take them to be pure aborigines if they were seen in Yucatan instead of Madras, Elephanta and other places of India.

If now we abandon that country and, crossing the Himalaya's range enter Afghanistan, there again we find ourselves in a country inhabited by Maya tribes; whose names, as those of many of their cities, are of pure American-Maya origin. In the fourth column of the sixth page of the London *Times*, weekly edition, of March 4, 1879, we read: "4,000 or 5,000 assembled on "the opposite bank of the river *Kabul*, and it appears "that in that day or evening they attacked the Maya "villages situated on the north side of the river."

He, the correspondent of the *Times*, tells us that Maya tribes form still part of the population of Afghanistan. He also tells us that *Kabul* is the name of the river, on the banks of which their villages are situated. But *Kabul* is the name of an antique shrine in the city of Izamal. Cogolludo, in the lib. IV., cap. VIII. of his History of Yucatan, says: "They had another temple on another mound, on the west side of the square, also dedicated to the same idol. They had there the symbol of a hand, as souvenir. To that temple they carried their dead and the sick. They called it *Kabul*, the working hand, and made there great offerings." Father Lizana says the same: so we have two witnesses to the fact. *Kab*, in Maya means hand; and *Bul* is to play at hazard.

Many of the names of places and towns of Afghanistan have not only a meaning in the American-Maya language, but are actually the same as those of places and villages in Yucatan to-day, for example :

The Valley of *Chenar* would be the valley of the *well of the woman's children—chen*, well, and *al*, the woman's children. The fertile valley of *Kunar* would be the valley of the *god of the ears of corn;* or, more probably, the *nest of the ears of corn*: as Kú, pronounced short, means *God*, and *Kuu*, pronounced long, is nest. NAL, is the *ears of corn*.

The correspondent of the London *Times*, in his letters, mentions the names of some of the principal tribes, such as the *Kuki-Khel*, the *Akakhel*, the *Khambhur Khel*, etc. The suffix Khel simply signifies tribe, or clan. So similar to the Maya vocable *Kaan*, a tie, a rope; hence a clan: a number of people held together by the tie of parentage. Now, Kuki would be Kukil, or Kukum, maya for feather, hence the KUKI-KHEL would be the tribe of the feather.

AKA-KHEL in the same manner would be the tribe of the reservoir, or pond. AKAL is the Maya name for the artificial reservoirs, or ponds in which the ancient inhabitants' of Mayab collected rain water for the time of drought.

Similarly the KHAMBHUR KHEL is the tribe of the *pleasant*: *Kambul* in Maya. It is the name of several villages of Yucatan, as you may satisfy yourself by examining the map.

We have also the ZAKA-KHEL, the tribe of the locust, ZAK. It is useless to quote more for the present: enough to say that if you read the names of the cities, valleys clans, roads even of Afghanistan to any of the aborigines of Yucatan, they will immediately give you their meaning in their own language. Before leaving the country of the Afghans, by the KHIBER Pass—that is to say, the *road of the hawk;* HI, *hawk*, and BEL, road— allow me to inform you that in examining their types, as published in the London illustrated papers, and in *Harper's Weekly*, I easily recognized the same cast of features as those of the bearded men, whose portraits we discovered in the bas-reliefs which adorn the antæ and pillars of the castle, and queen's box in the Tennis Court at Chichen-Itza.

On our way to the coast of Asia Minor, and hence to Egypt, we may, in following the Mayas' footsteps, notice that a tribe of them, the learned MAGI, with their Rabmag at their head, established themselves in Babylon, where they became, indeed, a powerful and influential body. Their chief they called *Rab-mag*—or LAB-MAC— the old person—LAB, *old*—MAC, person; and their name Magi, meant learned men, magicians, as that of Maya in India. I will directly speak more at length of vestiges of the Mayas in Babylon, when explaining by means of the *American Maya*, the meaning and probable etymology of the names of the Chaldaic divinities. At present I am trying to follow the footprints of the Mayas.

On the coast of Asia Minor we find a people of a roving and piratical disposition, whose name was, from the remotest antiquity and for many centuries, the terror of the populations dwelling on the shores of the Mediterranean; whose origin was, and is yet unknown; who must have spoken Maya, or some Maya dialect, since we find words of that language, and with the same meaning inserted in that of the Greeks, who, Herodotus tells us, used to laugh at the manner the *Carians*, or *Caras*, or *Carībs*, spoke their tongue; whose women wore a white linen dress that required no fastening, just as the Indian and Mestiza women of Yucatan even to-day

To tell you that the name of the CARAS is found over a vast extension of country in America, would be to repeat what the late and lamented Brasseur de Bourbourg has shown in his most learned introduction to the work of Landa, "Relacion de las cosas de Yucatan;" but this I may say, that the description of the customs and mode of life of the people of Yucatan, even at the time of the conquest, as written by Landa, seems to be a mere verbatim plagiarism of the description of the customs and mode of life of the Carians of Asia Minor by Herodotus.

If identical customs and manners, and the worship of the same divinities under the same name, besides the traditions of a people pointing towards a certain point of the globe as being the birth-place of their ancestors, prove anything, then I must say that in Egypt also we meet with the tracks of the Mayas, of whose name we again have a reminiscence in that of the goddess Maia, the daughter of Atlantis, worshiped in Greece. Here, at this end of the voyage, we seem to find an intimation as to the place where the Mayas originated. We are told that Maya is born from Atlantis; in other words, that the Mayas came from beyond the Atlantic waters. Here, also, we find that Maia is called the mother of the gods *Kubeles*. *Kú*, Maya *God*, *Bel* the road, the way. Ku-bel, the road, the origin of the gods as among the Hindostanees. These, we have seen in the Rig Veda, called Mâyâ, the feminine energy—the productive virtue of Brahma.

I do not pretend to present here anything but facts, resulting from my study of the ancient monuments of Yucatan, and a comparative study of the Maya language, in which the ancient inscriptions, I have been able to decipher, are written. Let us see if those *facts* are sustained by others of a different character.

I will make a brief parallel between the architectural monuments of the primitive Chaldeans, their mode of writing, their burial places, and give you the etymology of the names of their divinities in the American Maya language.

The origin of the primitive Chaldees is yet an unsettled matter among learned men. Some professing one opinion, others another. All agree, however, that they were strangers to the lower Mesopotamian valleys, where they settled in very remote ages, their capital being, in the time of Abraham, as we learn from Scriptures, *Ur* or *Hur*. So named either because its inhabitants were worshipers of the moon, or from the moon itself—u in the Maya language—or perhaps also because the founders being strangers and guests, as it were, in the country, it was called the city of guests, HULA (Maya), *guest just arrived*.

Recent researches in the plains of lower Mesopotamia have revealed to us their mode of building their sacred edifices, which is precisely identical to that of the Mayas.

It consisted of mounds composed of superposed platforms, either square or oblong, forming cones or pyramids, their angles at times, their faces at others, facing exactly the cardinal points.

Their manner of construction was also the same, with the exception of the materials employed—each people using those most at hand in their respective countries—clay and bricks in Chaldea, stones in Yucatan. The filling in of the buildings being of inferior materials, crude or sun-dried bricks at Warka and Mugheir; of unhewn stones of all shapes and sizes, in Uxmal and Chichen, faced with walls of hewn stones, many feet in thickness throughout. Grand exterior staircases lead to the summit, where was the shrine of the god, and temple.

In Yucatan these mounds are generally composed of seven superposed platforms, the one above being smaller than that immediately below; the temple or sanctuary containing invariably two chambers, the inner one, the Sanctum Sanctorum, being the smallest.

In Babylon, the supposed tower of Babel—the *Birs-i-nimrud*—the temple of the seven lights, was made of seven stages or platforms.

The roofs of these buildings in both countries were flat; the walls of vast thickness; the chambers long and narrow, with outer doors opening into them directly; the rooms ordinarily let into one another: squared recesses were common in the rooms. Mr. Loftus is of opinion that the chambers of the Chaldean buildings were usually arched with bricks, in which opinion Mr. Taylor concurs. We know that the ceilings of the chambers in all the monuments of Yucatan, without exception, form triangular arches. To describe their construction I will quote from the description by Herodotus, of some ceilings in Egyptian buildings and Scythian tombs, that resemble that of the brick vaults found at Mugheir. "The side walls slope "outward as they ascend, the arch is formed by each suc- "cessive layer of brick from the point where the arch "begins, a little overlapping the last, till the two sides "of the roof are brought so near together, that the aper- "ture may be closed by a single brick."

Some of the sepulchers found in Yucatan are very similar to the jar tombs common at Mugheir. These consist of two large open-mouthed jars, united with bitumen after the body has been deposited in them, with the usual accompaniments of dishes, vases and ornaments, having an air hole bored at one extremity. Those found at Progreso were stone urns about three feet square, cemented in pairs, mouth to mouth, and having also an air hole bored in the bottom. Extensive mounds, made artificially of a vast number of coffins, arranged side by side, divided by thin walls of masonry crossing each other at right angles, to separate the coffins, have been found in the lower plains of Chaldea—such as exist along the coast of Peru, and in Yucatan. At Izamal many human remains, contained in urns, have been found in the mounds.

"The ordinary dress of the common people among the Chaldeans," says Canon Rawlison, in his work, the Five Great Monarchies, "seems to have consisted of a single garment, a short tunic tied round the waist, and reaching thence to the knees. To this may sometimes have been added an *abba*, or cloak, thrown over the shoulders ; the material of the former we may perhaps presume to have been linen." The mural paintings at Chichen show that the Mayas sometimes used the same costume; and that dress is used to-day by the aborigines of Yucatan, and the inhabitants of the *Tierra de Guerra*. They were also bare-footed, and wore on the head a band of cloth, highly ornamented with mother-of-pearl instead of camel's hair, as the Chaldee. This band is to be seen in bas-relief at Chichen-Itza, in the mural paintings, and on the head of the statue of Chaacmol. The higher classes wore a long robe extending from the neck to the feet, sometimes adorned with a fringe; it appears not to have been fastened to the waist, but kept in place by passing over one shoulder, a slit or hole being made for the arm on one side of the dress only. In some cases the upper part of the dress seems to have been detached from the lower, and to form a sort of jacket which reached about to the hips. We again see this identical dress portrayed in the mural paintings. The same description of ornaments were affected by the Chaldees and the Mayas — bracelets, earrings, armlets, anklets, made of the materials they could procure.

The Mayas at times, as can be seen from the slab discovered by Bresseur in Mayapan (an exact fac-simile of which cast, from a mould made by myself, is now in the rooms of the American Antiquarian Society at Worcester, Mass.), as the primitive Chaldee, in their writings, made use of characters composed of straight lines only, inclosed in square or oblong figures; as we see from the inscriptions in what has been called hieratic form of writing found at Warka and Mugheir and the slab from Mayapan and others.

The Chaldees are said to have made use of three kinds of characters that Canon Rawlinson calls *letters proper*, *monograms* and *determinative*. The Maya also, as we see from the monumental inscriptions, employed three kinds of characters—*letters proper*, *monograms* and *pictorial*.

It may be said of the religion of the Mayas, as I have had occasion to remark, what the learned author of the Five Great Monarchies says of that of the primitive Chaldees: "The religion of the Chaldeans, from the very earliest times to which the monuments carry us back, was, in its outward aspect, a polytheism of a very elaborate character. It is quite possible that there may have been esoteric explanations, known to the priests and the more learned; which, resolving the personages of the Pantheon into the powers of nature, reconcile the apparent multiplicity of Gods with monotheism." I will now consider the names of the Chaldean deities in their turn of rotation as given us by the author above mentioned, and show you that the language of the American Mayas gives us an etymology of the whole of them, quite in accordance with their particular attributes.

RA.

The learned author places *Ra* at the head of the Pantheon, stating that the meaning of the word is simply *God*, or the God emphatically. We know that *Ra* was the Sun among the Egyptians, and that the hieroglyph, a circle, representation of that God was the same in Babylon as in Egypt. It formed an element in the native name of Babylon. Which was *ka-ra*.

Now the Mayas called LA, that which has existed for ever, the truth *par excellence*. As to the native name of Babylon it would simply be the *city of the infinite truth* —*cah*, city; LA, eternal truth.

ANA OR DIS.

Ana, like Ra, is thought to have signified *God* in the highest sense. Its etymology seems to be problematic. His epithets mark priority and antiquity; *the original chief*, the *father of the gods*, the *lord of darkness or death*. The Maya gives us A, *thy;* NA, *mother*. At times he was called DIS, and was the patron god of *Erech*, the great city of the dead, the necropolis of Lower Babylonia. TIX, Maya is a cavity formed in the earth. It seems to have given its name to the city of *Niffer*, called *Calneh* in the translation of the Septuagint, from *kal-ana*, which is translated the "fort of Ana;" or according to the Maya, the *prison of Ana*, KAL being prison, or the prison of thy mother.

ANATA

the supposed wife of Ana, has no peculiar characteristics. Her name is only, says our author, the feminine form of the masculine, Ana. But the Maya designates her as the companion of Ana; TA, with; *Anata* with *Ana*.

BIL OR ENU

seems to mean merely Lord. It is usually followed by a qualificative adjunct, possessing great interest, NIPRU. To that name, which recalls that of NEBROTH or *Nimrod*, the author gives a Syriac etymology; napar (make to flee). His epithets are the *supreme, the father of the gods*, the *procreator*.

The Maya gives us BIL, or *Bel;* the way, the road; hence the *origin*, the father, the procreator. Also ENA, who is before; again the father, the procreator.

As to the qualificative adjunct *nipru*. It would seem to be the Maya *niblu*; *nib*, to thank; LU, the *Bagre*, a *silurus fish*. *Niblu* would then be the *thanksgiving fish*. Strange to say, the high priest at Uxmal and Chichen, elder brother of Chaacmol, first son of *Can*, the founder of those cities, is CAY, the fish, whose effigy is my last discovery in June, among the ruins of Uxmal. The bust is contained within the jaws of a serpent, *Can*, and over it, is a beautiful mastodon head, with the trunk inscribed with Egyptian characters, which read TZAA, that which is necessary.

BELTIS

is the wife of *Bel-nipru*. But she is more than his mere female power. She is a separate and important deity. Her common title is the *Great Goddess*. In Chaldea her name was *Mulita* or *Enuta*, both words signifying the lady. Her favorite title was the *mother of the gods*, the origin of the gods.

In Maya BEL is the road, the way; and TE means *here*. BELTÉ or BELTIS would be I am the way, the origin.

Mulita would correspond to MUL-TE, many here, *many in me*. I am the mother of many. Her other name *Enuta* seems to be (Maya) *Ena-te*, signifies ENA, the first, before anybody, and TE here. ENATÉ, I *am here before anybody*, I am the mother of the Gods.

HEA OR HOA.

The God Fish, the mystic animal, half man, half fish, which came up from the Persian gulf to teach astronomy and letters to the first settlers on the Euphrates and Tigris.

According to Berosus the civilization was brought to Mesopotamia by *Oannes* and six other beings, who, like himself, were half man, half fish, and that they came from the Indian Ocean. We have already seen that the Mayas of India were not only architects, but also astronomers; and the symbolic figure of a being half man and half fish seems to clearly indicate that those who brought civilization to the shores of the Euphrates and Tigris came in boats.

Hoa-Ana, or Oannes, according to the Maya would mean, he who has his residence or house on the water. HA, being water; *a*, thy; *ná*, house; literally, *water thy house*. Canon Rawlison remarks in that connection:

"There are very strong grounds for connecting HEA or "Hoa, with the serpent of the Scripture, and the para- "disaical traditions of the tree of knowledge and the tree "of life." As the title of the god of knowledge and science, *Oannes*, is the lord of the abyss, or of the great deep, the intelligent fish, one of his emblems being the serpent, CAN, which occupies so conspicuous a place among the symbols of the gods on the black stones recording benefactions.

DAV-KINA

Is the wife of *Hoa*, and her name is thought to signify the chief lady. But the Maya again gives us another meaning that seems to me more appropriate. TAB-KIN would be the *rays of the sun:* the rays of the light brought with civilization by her husband to benighted inhabitants of Mesopotamia.

SIN OR HURKI

is the name of the moon deity; the etymology of it is quite uncertain. Its titles, as Rawlison remarks, are somewhat vague. Yet it is particularly designated as "*the bright, the shining,*" the lord of the month.

Zin in Maya has also many significations. Zin is to stretch, to extend. *Zinil* is the extension of the whole of the universe. *Hurki* would be the Maya HULKIN— sun-stroked; he who receives directly the rays of the sun. Hurki is also the god presiding over buildings and architecture; in this connection he is called *Bel-Zuna.* The *lord of building*, the *supporting architect*, the *strengthener of fortifications.* Bel-Zuna would also signify the lord of the strong house. *Zuú*, Maya, close, thick. *Na*, house: and the city where he had his great temple was *Ur*; named after him. *U*, in Maya, signifies moon.

SAN OR SANSI,

the Sun God, the *lord of fire*, the *ruler of the day.* He *who illumines the expanse of heaven and earth.*

Zamal (Maya) is the morning, the dawn of the day, and his symbols are the same on the temples of Yucatan as on those of Chaldea, India and Egypt.

VUL OR IVA,

the prince of the powers of the air, the lord of the whirlwind and the tempest, the wielder of the thunderbolt, the lord of the air, he who makes the tempest to rage. • *Hiba* in Maya is to rub, to scour, to chafe as does the tempest. As VUL he is represented with a flaming sword in his hand. *Hul* (Maya) an arrow. He is then the god of the atmosphere, who gives rain.

ISHTAR OR NANA,

the Chaldean Venus, of the etymology of whose name no satisfactory account can be given, says the learned author, whose list I am following and description quoting.

The Maya language, however, affords a very natural etymology. Her name seems composed of *ix*, the feminine article, *she*; and of *tac*, or *tal*, a verb that signifies to have a desire to satisfy a corporal want or inclination. IXTAL would, therefore, be she who desires to satisfy a corporal inclination. As to her other name, *Nana*, it simply means the great mother, the very mother. If from the names of god and goddesses, we pass to that of places, we will find that the Maya language also furnishes a perfect etymology for them.

In the account of the creation of the world, according to the Chaldeans, we find that a woman whose name in Chaldee is *Thalatth*, was said to have ruled over the monstrous animals of strange forms, that were generated and existed in darkness and water. The Greek called her *Thalassa* (the sea). But the Maya vocable *Thallac*, signifies a thing without steadiness, like the sea.

URUKH.

The first king of the Chaldees was a great architect. To him are ascribed the most archaic monuments of the plains of Lower Mesopotamia. He is said to have conceived the plans of the Babylonian Temple. He constructed his edifices of mud and bricks, with rectangular bases, their angles fronting the cardinal points; receding stages, exterior staircases, with shrines crowning the whole structure. In this description of the primitive constructions of the Chaldeans, no one can fail to recognize the Maya mode of building, and we see them not only in Yucatan, but throughout Central America, Peru, even Hindoostan. The very name *Urkuh* seems composed of two Maya words HUK, to make everything, and LUK, mud; he who makes everything of mud; so significative of his building propensities and of the materials used by him.

ASSYRIA.

The etymology of the name of that country, as well as that of Asshur, the supreme god of the Assyrians, who never pronounced his name without adding "Asshur is my lord," is still an undecided matter amongst the learned philologists of our days. Some contend that the country was named after the god Asshur; others that the god Asshur received his name from the place where he was worshiped. None agree, however, as to the significative meaning of the name Asshur. In Assyrian and Hebrew languages the name of the country and people is derived from that of the god. That Asshur was the name of the deity, and that the country was named after it, I have no doubt, since I find its etymology, so much sought for by philologists, in the American Maya language. Effectively the word *asshur*, sometimes written *ashur*, would be AXUL in Maya.

A, in that language, placed before a noun, is the possessive pronoun, as the second person, thy or thine, and *xul*, means end, termination. It is also the name of the sixth month of the Maya calendar. *Axul* would therefore be *thy end*. Among all the nations which have recognized the existence of a SUPREME BEING, Deity has been considered as the beginning and end of all things, to which all aspire to be united.

A strange coincidence that may be without significance, but is not out of place to mention here, is the fact that the early kings of Chaldea are represented on the monuments as sovereigns over the *Kiprat-arbat*, or FOUR RACES. While tradition tells us that the great lord of the universe, king of the giants, whose capital was *Tiahuanaco*, the magnificent ruins of which are still to be seen on the shores of the lake of Titicaca, reigned over *Tlahuatyn-suyu*, the FOUR PROVINCES. In the *Chou-King* we read that in very remote times *China* was called by its inhabitants *Sse-yo*, THE FOUR PARTS OF THE EMPIRE. The *Manava-Dharma-Sastra*, the *Ramayana*, and other sacred books of Hindostan also inform us that the ancient Hindoos designated their country as the FOUR MOUNTAINS, and from some of the monumental inscriptions at Uxmal it would seem that, among other names, that place was called the land of the *canchi*, or FOUR MOUTHS, that recalls vividly the name of Chaldea *Arba-Lisun*, the FOUR TONGUES.

That the language of the Mayas was known in Chaldea in remote ages, but became lost in the course of time, is evident from the Book of Daniel. It seems that some of the learned men of Judea understood it still at the beginning of the Christian era, as many to-day understand Greek, Latin, Sanscrit, &c.; since, we are informed by the writers of the Gospels of St. Matthew and St. Mark, that the last words of Jesus of Nazareth expiring on the cross were uttered in it.

In the fifth chapter of the Book of Daniel, we read that the fingers of the hand of a man were seen writing on the wall of the hall, where King Belshazzar was banqueting, the words "Mene, mene, Tekel, upharsin," which could not be read by any of the wise men summoned by order of the king. Daniel, however, being brought in, is said to have given as their interpretation: *Numbered, numbered, weighed, dividing*, perhaps with the help of the angel Gabriel, who is said by learned rabbins to be the only individual of the angelic hosts who can speak Chaldean and Syriac, and had once before assisted him in interpreting the dream of King Nebuchadnezzar. Perhaps also, having been taught the learning of the Chaldeans, he had studied the ancient Chaldee language, and was thus enabled to read the fatidical words, which have the very same meaning in the Maya language as he gave them. Effectively, *mene* or *mane*, *numbered*, would seem to correspond to the Maya verbs, MAN, to buy, to purchase, hence to number, things being sold by the quantity — or MANEL, to pass, to exceed. *Tekel*, weighed, would correspond to TEC, light. To-day it is used in the sense of lightness in motion, brevity, nimbleness: and *Upharsin*, dividing, seem allied to the words PPA, to divide two things united; or *uppah*, to break, making a sharp sound; or *paah*, to break edifices; or, again, PAALTAL, to break, to scatter the inhabitants of a place.

As to the last words of Jesus of Nazareth, when expiring on the cross, as reported by the Evangelists, *Eli, Eli,* according to St. Matthew, and *Eloi, Eloi,* according to St. Mark, *lama sabachthani,* they are pure Maya vocables; but have a very different meaning to that attributed to them, and more in accordance with His character. By placing in the mouth of the dying martyr these words: *My God, my God, why hast thou forsaken me?* they have done him an injustice, presenting him in his last moments despairing and cowardly, traits so foreign to his life, to his teachings, to the resignation shown by him during his trial, and to the fortitude displayed by him in his last journey to Calvary; more than all, so unbecoming, not to say absurd, being in glaring contradiction to his role as God. If God himself, why complain that God has forsaken him? He evidently did not speak Hebrew in dying, since his two mentioned biographers inform us that the people around him did not understand what he said, and supposed he was calling Elias to help him: *This man calleth for Elias.*

His bosom friend, who never abandoned him—who stood to the last at the foot of the cross, with his mother and other friends and relatives, do not report such unbefitting words as having been uttered by Jesus. He simply says, that after recommending his mother to his care, he complained of being thirsty, and that, as the sponge saturated with vinegar was applied to his mouth, he merely said : IT IS FINISHED ! and *he bowed his head and gave up the ghost.* (St. John, chap. xix., v. 30.)

Well, this is exactly the meaning of the Maya words, HELO, HELO, LAMAH ZABAC TA NI, literally : HELO, HELO, now, now ; LAMAH, sinking ; ZABAC, black ink ; TA, over; NI, nose ; in our language : *Now, now I am sinking ; darkness covers my face !* No weakness, no despair—He merely tells his friends all is over. *It is finished !* and expires.

Before leaving Asia Minor, in order to seek in Egypt the vestiges of the Mayas, I will mention the fact that the names of some of the natives who inhabited of old that part of the Asiatic continent, and many of those of places and cities seem to be of American Maya origin. The Promised Land, for example—that part of the coast of Phœnicia so famous for the fertility of its soil, where the Hebrews, after journeying during forty years in the desert, arrived at last, tired and exhausted from so many hard-fought battles—was known as *Canaan.* This is a Maya word that means to be tired, to be fatigued ; and, if it is spelled *Kanaan*, it then signifies abundance ; both significations applying well to the country.

TYRE, the great emporium of the Phœnicians, called *Tzur*, probably on account of being built on a rock, may also derive its name from the Maya *Tzuc*, a promontory, or a number of villages, *Tzucub* being a province.

Again, we have the people called *Khati* by the Egyptians. They formed a great nation that inhabited the *Cœle-Syria* and the valley of the Orontes, where they have left very interesting proofs of their passage on earth, in large and populous cities whose ruins have been lately discovered. Their origin is unknown, and is yet a problem to be solved. They are celebrated on account of their wars against the Assyrians and Egyptians, who call them the plague of Khati. Their name is frequently mentioned in the Scriptures as Hittites. Placed on the road, between the Assyrians and the Egyptians, by whom they were at last vanquished, they placed well nigh insuperable *obstacles in the way* of the conquests of these two powerful nations, which found in them tenacious and fearful adversaries. The Khati had not only made considerable improvements in all military arts, but were also great and famed merchants; their emporium *Carchemish* had no less importance than Tyre or Carthage. There, met merchants from all parts of the world; who brought thither the products and manufactures of their respective countries, and were wont to worship at the Sacred City, *Katish* of the Khati. The etymology of their name is also unknown. Some historians having pretended that they were a Scythian tribe, derived it from Scythia; but I think that we may find it very natural, as that of their principal cities, in the Maya language.

All admit that the Khati, until the time when they were vanquished by Rameses the Great, as recorded on the walls of his palace at Thebes, the *Memnonium*, always placed obstacles on the way of the Egyptians and opposed them. According to the Maya, their name is significative of these facts, since KAT or KATAH is a verb that means to place impediments on the road, to come forth and obstruct the passage.

Carchemish was their great emporium, where merchants from afar congregated; it was consequently a city of merchants. CAH means a city, and *Chemul* is navigator. *Carchemish* would then be *cah-chemul*, the city of navigators, of merchants.

KATISH, their sacred city, would be the city where sacrifices are offered. CAH, city, and TICH, a ceremony practiced by the ancient Mayas, and still performed by their descendants all through Central America. This sacrifice or ceremony consists in presenting to BALAM, the *Yumil-Kaax*, the "Lord of the fields," the *primitiæ* of all their fruits before beginning the harvest. Katish, or *cah-tich* would then be the city of the sacrifices—the holy city.

EGYPT is the country that in historical times has called, more than any other, the attention of the students, of all nations and in all ages, on account of the grandeur and beauty of its monuments; the peculiarity of its inhabitants; their advanced civilization, their great attainments in all branches of human knowledge and industry; and its important position at the head of all other nations of antiquity. Egypt has been said to be the source from which human knowledge began to flow over the old world: yet no one knows for a certainty whence came the people that laid the first foundations of that interesting nation. That they were not autochthones is certain. Their learned priests pointed towards the regions of the West as the birth-place of their ancestors, and designated the country in which they lived, the East, as the *pure land*, the *land of the sun*, of *light*, in contradistinction of the country of the dead, of darkness—the Amenti, the West —where Osiris sat as King, reigning judge, over the souls.

If in Hindostan, Afghanistan, Chaldea, Asia Minor, we have met with vestiges of the Mayas, in Egypt we will find their traces everywhere. Whatever may have been the name given to the valley watered by the Nile by its primitive inhabitants, no one at present knows. The invaders that came from the West called it CHEM: not on account of the black color of the soil, as Plutarch pretends in his work, "*De Iside et Osiride*," but more likely because either they came to it in boats; or, quite probably, because when they arrived the country was inundated, and the inhabitants communicated by means of boats, causing the new comers to call it the country of boats—CHEM (maya). The hieroglyph representing the name of Egypt is composed of the character used for land, a cross circumscribed by a circle, and of another, read K, which represent a sieve, it is said, but that may likewise be the picture of a small boat. The Assyrians designated Egypt under the names of MISIR or MISUR, probably because the country is generally destitute of trees. These are uprooted during the inundations, and then carried by the currents all over the country; so that the farmers, in order to be able to plow the soil, are obliged to clear it first from the dead trees. Now we have the Maya verb MIZ—to *clean*, to *remove rubbish formed by the body of dead trees;* whilst the verb MUSUR means to *cut the trees by the roots.* It would seem that the name *Mizraim* given to Egypt in the Scriptures also might come from these words.

When the Western invaders reached the country it was probably covered by the waters of the river, to which, we are told, they gave the name of *Hapimú.* Its etymology seems to be yet undecided by the Egyptologists, who agree, however, that its meaning is the *abyss of water.* The Maya tells us that this name is composed of two words—HÁ, water, and PIMIL, the thickness of flat things. *Hapimu,* or HAPIMIL, would then be the thickness, the *abyss of water.*

We find that the prophets *Jeremiah* (xlvi., 25,) and *Nahum* (iii., 8, 10,) call THEBES, the capital of upper Egypt during the XVIII. dynasty: NÓ or NÁ-AMUN, the mansion of Amun. *Ná* signifies in Maya, house, mansion, residence. But *Thebes* is written in Egyptian hieroglyphs AP, or APÉ, the meaning of which is the head, the capital; with the feminine article T, that is always used as its prefix in hieroglyphic writings, it becomes TAPÉ; which, according to Sir Gardner Wilkinson ("Manners and Customs of the Ancient Egyptians," *tom.* III., page 210, N. Y. Edition, 1878), was pronounced by the Egyptians *Taba;* and in the Menphitic dialect Thaba, that the Greeks converted into Thebai, whence Thebes. The Maya verb *Teppal,* signifies to reign, to govern, to order. On each side of the mastodons' heads, which form so prominent a feature in the ornaments of the oldest edifices at Uxmal, Chichen-Itza and other parts, the word *Dapas;* hence TABAS is written in ancient Egyptian characters, and read, I presume, in old Maya, *head.* To-day the word is pronounced THAB, and means *baldness.*

The identity of the names of deities worshiped by individuals, of their religious rites and belief; that of the names of the places which they inhabit; the similarity of their customs, of their dresses and manners; the sameness of their scientific attainments and of the characters used by them in expressing their language in writing, lead us naturally to infer that they have had a common origin, or, at least, that their forefathers were intimately connected. If we may apply this inference to nations likewise, regardless of the distance that to-day separates the countries where they live, I can then affirm that the Mayas and the Egyptians are either of a common descent, or that very intimate communication must have existed in remote ages between their ancestors.

Without entering here into a full detail of the customs and manners of these people, I will make a rapid comparison between their religious belief, their customs, manners, scientific attainments, and the characters used by them in writing etc., sufficient to satisfy any reasonable body that the strange coincidences that follow, cannot be altogether accidental.

The SUN, RA, was the supreme god worshiped throughout the land of Egypt; and its emblem was a disk or circle, at times surmounted by the serpent Uræus. Egypt was frequently called the Land of the Sun. RA or LA signifies in Maya that which exists, emphatically that which is—the truth.

The sun was worshiped by the ancient Mayas; and the Indians to-day preserve the dance used by their forefathers among the rites of the adoration of that luminary, and perform it yet in certain epoch of the year. The coat-of-arms of the city of Uxmal, sculptured on the west façade of the sanctuary, attached to the masonic temple in that city, teaches us that the place was called U LUUMIL KIN, *the land of the sun*. This name forming the center of the escutcheon, is written with a cross, circumscribed by a circle, that among the Egyptians is the sign for land, region, surrounded by the rays of the sun.

Colors in Egypt, as in Mayab, seem to have had the same symbolical meaning. The figure of *Amun* was that of a man whose body was light blue, like the Indian god Wishnu, and that of the god Nilus; as if to indicate their peculiar exalted and heavenly nature; this color being that of the pure, bright skies above. The blue color had exactly the same significance in Mayab, according to Landa and Cogolludo, who tell us that, even at the time of the Spanish conquest, the bodies of those who were to be sacrificed to the gods were painted blue. The mural paintings in the funeral chamber of Chaacmol, at Chichen, confirm this assertion. There we see figures of men and women painted blue, some marching to the sacrifice with their hands tied behind their backs. After being thus painted they were venerated by the people, who regarded them as sanctified. Blue in Egypt was always the color used at the funerals.

The Egyptians believed in the immortality of the soul; and that rewards and punishments were adjudged by Osiris, the king of the Amenti, to the souls according to their deeds during their mundane life. That the souls after a period of three thousand years were to return to earth and inhabit again their former earthly tenements. This was the reason why they took so much pains to embalm the body.

The Mayas also believed in the immortality of the soul, as I have already said. Their belief was that after the spirit had suffered during a time proportioned to their misdeeds whilst on earth, and after having enjoyed an amount of bliss corresponding to their good actions, they were to return to earth and live again a material life. Accordingly, as the body was corruptible, they made statues of stones, terra-cotta, or wood, in the semblance of the deceased, whose ashes they deposited in a hollow made for that purpose in the back of the head. Sometimes also in stone urns, as in the case of Chaacmol. The spirits, on their return to earth, were to find these statues, impart life to them, and use them as body during their new existence.

I am not certain but that, as the Egyptians also, they were believers in transmigration; and that this belief exists yet among the aborigines. I have noticed that my Indians were unwilling to kill any animal whatever, even the most noxious and dangerous, that inhabits the ruined monuments. I have often told them to kill some venomous insect or serpent that may have happened to be in our way. They invariably refused to do so, but softly and carefully caused them to go. And when asked why they did not kill them, declined to answer except by a knowing and mysterious smile, as if afraid to let a stranger into their intimate beliefs inherited from their ancestors: remembering, perhaps, the fearful treatment inflicted by fanatical friars on their fathers to oblige them to forego what they called the superstitions of their race—the idolatrous creed of their forefathers.

I have had opportunity to discover that their faith in reincarnation, as many other time-honored credences, still exists among them, unshaken, notwithstanding the persecutions and tortures suffered by them at the hands of ignorant and barbaric *Christians* (?)

I will give two instances when that belief in reincarnation was plainly manifested.

The day that, after surmounting many difficulties, when my ropes and cables, made of withes and the bark of the *habin* tree, were finished and adjusted to the capstan manufactured of hollow stones and trunks of trees; and I had placed the ponderous statue of Chaacmol on rollers, already in position to drag it up the inclined plane made from the surface of the ground to a few feet above the bottom of the excavation; my men, actuated by their superstitious fears on the one hand, and their profound reverence for the memory of their ancestors on the other, unwilling to see the effigy of one of the great men removed from where their ancestors had placed it in ages gone by resolved to bury it, by letting loose the hill of dry stones that formed the body of the mausoleum, and were kept from falling in the hole by a framework of thin trunks of trees tied with withes, and in order that it should not be injured, to capsize it, placing the face downward. They had already overturned it, when I interfered in time to prevent more mischief, and even save some of them from certain death; since by cutting loose the withes that keep the framework together, the sides of the excavation were bound to fall in, and crush those at the bottom. I honestly think, knowing their superstitious feelings and propensities, that they had made up their mind to sacrifice their lives, in order to avoid what they considered a desecration of the future tenement that the great warrior and king was yet to inhabit, when time had arrived. In order to overcome their scruples, and also to prove if my suspicions were correct, that, as their forefathers and the Egyptians of old, they still believed in reincarnation, I caused them to accompany me to the summit of the great pyramid. There is a monument, that served as a castle when the city of the holy men, the Itzaes, was at the height of its splendor. Every anta, every pillar and column of this edifice is sculptured with portraits of warriors and noblemen. Among these many with long beards, whose types recall vividly to the mind the features of the Afghans.

On one of the antæ, at the entrance on the north side, is the portrait of a warrior wearing a long, straight, pointed beard. The face, like that of all the personages represented in the bas-reliefs, is in profile. I placed my head against the stone so as to present the same position of my face as that of UXAN, and called the attention of my Indians to the similarity of his and my own features.

They followed every lineament of the faces with their fingers to the very point of the beard, and soon uttered an exclamation of astonishment: "*Thou! here!*" and slowly scanned again the features sculptured on the stone and my own.

"*So, so,*" they said, "*thou too art one of our great men, who has been disenchanted. Thou, too, wert a companion of the great Lord Chaacmol. That is why thou didst know where he was hidden; and thou hast come to disenchant him also. His time to live again on earth has then arrived.*"

From that moment every word of mine was implicitly obeyed. They returned to the excavation, and worked with such a good will, that they soon brought up the ponderous statue to the surface.

A few days later some strange people made their appearance suddenly and noiselessly in our midst. They emerged from the thicket one by one. Colonel *Don Felipe Diaz*, then commander of the troops covering the eastern frontier, had sent me, a couple of days previous, a written notice, that I still preserve in my power, that tracks of hostile Indians had been discovered by his scouts, advising me to keep a sharp look out, lest they should surprise us. Now, to be on the look out in the midst of a thick, well-nigh impenetrable forest, is a rather difficult thing to do, particularly with only a few men, and where there is no road; yet all being a road for the enemy. Warning my men that danger was near, and to keep their loaded rifles at hand, we continued our work as usual, leaving the rest to destiny.

On seeing the strangers, my men rushed on their weapons, but noticing that the visitors had no guns, but only their *machetes*, I gave orders not to hurt them. At their head was a very old man: his hair was gray, his eyes blue with age. He would not come near the statue, but stood at a distance as if awe-struck, hat in hand, looking at it. After a long time he broke out, speaking to his own people: "This, boys, is one of the great men we speak to you about." Then the young men came forward, with great respect kneeled at the feet of the statue, and pressed their lips against them.

Putting aside my own weapons, being consequently unarmed, I went to the old man, and asked him to accompany me up to the castle, offering my arm to ascend the 100 steep and crumbling stairs. I again placed my face near that of my stone *Sosis*, and again the same scene was enacted as with my own men, with this difference, that the strangers fell on their knees before me, and, in turn, kissed my hand. The old man after a while, eyeing me respectfully, but steadily, asked me: "Rememberest thou what happened to thee whilst thou wert enchanted?" It was quite a difficult question to answer, and yet retain my superior position, for I did not know how many people might be hidden in the thicket. "Well, father," I asked him, "dreamest thou sometimes?" He nodded his head in an affirmative manner. "And when thou awakest, dost thou remember distinctly thy dreams?" "*Má*," no! was the answer. "Well, father," I continued, "so it happened with me. I do not remember what took place during the time I was enchanted." This answer seemed to satisfy him. I again gave him my hand to help him down the precipitous stairs, at the foot of which we separated, wishing them God-speed, and warning them not to go too near the villages on their way back to their homes, as people were aware of their presence in the country. Whence they came, I ignore; where they went, I don't know.

Circumcision was a rite in usage among the Egyptians since very remote times. The Mayas also practiced it, if we are to credit Fray Luis de Urreta; yet Cogolludo affirms that in his days the Indians denied observing such custom. The outward sign of utmost reverence seems to have been identical amongst both the Mayas and the Egyptians. It consisted in throwing the left arm across the chest, resting the left hand on the right shoulder; or the right arm across the chest, the right hand resting on the left shoulder. Sir Gardner Wilkinson, in his work above quoted, reproduces various figures in that attitude; and Mr. Champollion Figeac, in his book on Egypt, tells us that in some cases even the mummies of certain eminent men were placed in their coffins with the arms in that position. That this same mark of respect was in use amongst the Mayas there can be no possible doubt. We see it in the figures represented in the act of worshiping the mastodon's head, on the west façade of the monument that forms the north wing of the palace and museum at Chichen-Itza. We see it repeatedly in the mural paintings in Chaacmol's funeral chamber; on the slabs sculptured with the representation of a dying warrior, that adorned the mausoleum of that chieftain. Cogolludo mentions it in his history of Yucatan, as being common among the aborigines: and my own men have used it to show their utmost respect to persons or objects they consider worthy of their veneration. Among my collection of photographs are several plates in which some of the men have assumed that position of the arms spontaneously.

The sistrum was an instrument used by Egyptians and Mayas alike during the performance of their religious rites and acts of worship. I have seen it used lately by natives in Yucatan in the dance forming part of the worship of the sun. The Egyptians enclosed the brains, entrails and viscera of the deceased in funeral vases, called *canopas*, that were placed in the tombs with the coffin. When I opened Chaacmol's mausoleum I found, as I have already said, two stone urns, the one near the head containing the remains of brains, that near the chest those of the heart and other viscera. This fact would tend to show again a similar custom among the Mayas and Egyptians, who, besides, placed with the body an empty vase—symbol that the deceased had been judged and found righteous. This vase, held between the hands of the statue of Chaacmol, is also found held in the same manner by many other statues of different individuals. It was customary with the Egyptians to deposit in the tombs the implements of the trade or profession of the deceased. So also with the Mayas—if a priest, they placed books; if a warrior, his weapons; if a mechanic, the tools of his art,

The Egyptians adorned the tombs of the rich—which generally consisted of one or two chambers—with sculptures and paintings reciting the names and the history of the life of the personage to whom the tomb belonged. The mausoleum of Chaacmol, interiorly, was composed of three different superposed apartments, with their floors of concrete well leveled, polished and painted with yellow ochre; and exteriorly was adorned with magnificent bas-reliefs, representing his totem and that of his wife—dying warriors—the whole being surrounded by the image of a feathered serpent—*Can*, his family name, whilst the walls of the two apartments, or funeral chambers, in the monument raised to his memory, were decorated with fresco paintings, representing not only Chaacmol's own life, but the manners, customs, mode of dressing of his contemporaries; as those of the different nations with which they were in communication: distinctly recognizable by their type, stature and other peculiarities. The portraits of the great and eminent men of his time are sculptured on the jambs and lintels of the doors, represented life-size.

In Egypt it was customary to paint the sculptures, either on stone or wood, with bright colors—yellow, blue, red, green predominating. In Mayab the same custom prevailed, and traces of these colors are still easily discernible on the sculptures; whilst they are still very brilliant on the beautiful and highly polished stucco of the walls in the rooms of certain monuments at Chichen-Itza. The Maya artists seem to have used mostly vegetable colors; yet they also employed ochres as pigments, and cinnabar—we having found such metallic colors in Chaacmol's mausoleum. Mrs. Le Plongeon still preserves some in her possession. From where they procured it is more than we can tell at present.

The wives and daughters of the Egyptian kings and noblemen considered it an honor to assist in the temples and religious ceremonies: one of their principal duties being to play the sistrum.

We find that in Yucatan, *Nicté* (flower) the sister of *Chaacmol*, assisted her elder brother, *Cay*, the pontiff, in the sanctuary, her name being always associated with his in the inscriptions which adorn the western façade of that edifice at Uxmal, as that of her sister, *Mó*, is with Chaacmol's in some of the monuments at Chichen.

Cogolludo, when speaking of the priestesses, *virgins of the sun*, mentions a tradition that seems to refer to *Nicté*, stating that the daughter of a king, who remained during all her life in the temple, obtained after her death the honor of apotheosis, and was worshiped under the name of *Zuhuy-Kak* (the fire-virgin), and became the goddess of the maidens, who were recommended to her care.

As in Egypt, the kings and heroes were worshiped in Mayab after their death; temples and pyramids being raised to their memory. Cogolludo pretends that the lower classes adored fishes, snakes, tigers and other abject animals, "even the devil himself, which appeared to them in horrible forms" ("Historia de Yucatan," book IV., chap. vii.)

Judging from the sculptures and mural paintings, the higher classes in *Mayab* wore, in very remote ages, dresses of quite an elaborate character. Their under garment consisted of short trowsers, reaching the middle of the thighs. At times these trowsers were highly ornamented with embroideries and fringes, as they formed their only article of clothing when at home; over these they wore a kind of kilt, very similar to that used by the inhabitants of the Highlands in Scotland. It was fastened to the waist with wide ribbons, tied behind in a knot forming a large bow, the ends of which reached to the ankles. Their shoulders were covered with a tippet falling to the elbows, and fastened on the chest by means of a brooch. Their feet were protected by sandals, kept in place by ropes or ribbons, passing between the big toe and the next, and between the third and fourth, then brought up so as to encircle the ankles. They were tied in front, forming a bow on the instep. Some wore leggings, others garters and anklets made of feathers, generally yellow; sometimes, however, they may have been of gold. Their head gears were of different kinds, according to their rank and dignity. Warriors seem to have used wide bands, tied behind the head with two knots, as we see in the statue of Chaacmol, and in the bas-reliefs that adorn the queen's chamber at Chichen. The king's coiffure was a peaked cap, that seems to have served as model for the *pschent*, that symbol of domination over the lower Egypt; with this difference, however, that in Mayab the point formed the front, and in Egypt the back.

The common people in Mayab, as in Egypt, were indeed little troubled by their garments. These consisted merely of a simple girdle tied round the loins, the ends falling before and behind to the middle of the thighs. Sometimes they also used the short trowsers; and, when at work. wrapped a piece of cloth round their loins, long enough to cover their legs to the knees. This costume was completed by wearing a square cloth, tied on one of the shoulders by two of its corners. It served as cloak. To-day the natives of Yucatan wear the same dress, with but slight modifications. While the aborigines of the *Tierra de Guerra*, who still preserve the customs of their forefathers, untainted by foreign admixture, use the same garments, of their own manufacture, that we see represented in the bas-reliefs of Chichen and Uxmal, and in the mural paintings of *Mayab* and Egypt.

Divination by the inspection of the entrails of victims, and the study of omens were considered by the Egyptians as important branches of learning. The soothsayers formed a respected order of the priesthood. From the mural paintings at Chichen, and from the works of the chroniclers, we learn that the Mayas also had several manners of consulting fate. One of the modes was by the inspection of the entrails of victims; another by the manner of the cracking of the shell of a turtle or armadillo by the action of fire, as among the Chinese. (In the *Hong-fan* or "the great and sublime doctrine," one of the books of the *Chou-king*, the ceremonies of *Pou* and *Chi* are described at length). The Mayas had also their astrologers and prophets. Several prophecies, purporting to have been made by their priests, concerning the preaching of the Gospel among the people of Mayab, have reached us, preserved in the works of Landa, Lizana, and Cogolludo. There we also read that, even at the time of the Spanish conquest, they came from all parts of the country, and congregated at the shrine of *Kinich-kakmo*, the deified daughter of CAN, to listen to the oracles delivered by her through the mouths of her priests and consult her on future events. By the examination of the mural paintings, we know that *animal magnetism* was understood and practiced by the priests, who, themselves, seem to have consulted clairvoyants.

The learned priests of Egypt are said to have made considerable progress in astronomical sciences.

The *gnomon*, discovered by me in December, last year, in the ruined city of Mayapan, would tend to prove that the learned men of Mayab were not only close observers of the march of the celestial bodies and good mathematicians; but that their attainments in astronomy were not inferior to those of their brethren of Chaldea. Effectively the construction of the gnomon shows that they had found the means of calculating the latitude of places, that they knew the distance of the solsticeal points from the equator; they had found that the greatest angle of declination of the sun, 23° 27′, occurred when that luminary reached the tropics where, during nearly three days, said angle of declination does not vary, for which reason they said that the *sun* had arrived at his resting place.

The Egyptians, it is said, in very remote ages, divided the year by lunations, as the Mayas, who divided their civil year into eighteen months, of twenty days, that they called U—moon—to which they added five supplementary days, that they considered unlucky. From an epoch so ancient that it is referred to the fabulous time of their history, the Egyptians adopted the solar year, dividing it into twelve months, of thirty days, to which they added, at the end of the last month, called *Mesoré*, five days, named *Epact*.

By a most remarkable coincidence, the Egyptians, as the Mayas, considered these additive five days *unlucky*.

Besides this solar year they had a sideral or sothic year, composed of 365 days and 6 hours, which corresponds exactly to the Mayas sacred year, that Landa tells us was also composed of 365 days and 6 hours; which they represented in the gnomon of Mayapan by the line that joins the centers of the stela that forms it.

The Egyptians, in their computations, calculated by a system of *fives* and *tens;* the Mayas by a system of *fives* and *twenties*, to four hundred. Their sacred number appears to have been 13 from the remotest antiquity, but SEVEN seems to have been a *mystic number* among them as among the Hindoos, Aryans, Chaldeans, Egyptians, and other nations.

The Egyptians made use of a septenary system in the arrangement of the grand gallery in the center of the great pyramid. Each side of the wall is made of seven courses of finely polished stones, the one above overlapping that below, thus forming the triangular ceiling common to all the edifices in Yucatan. This gallery is said to be seven times the height of the other passages, and, as all the rooms in Uxmal, Chichen and other places in Mayab, it is seven-sided. Some authors pretend to assume that this well marked septenary system has reference to the *Pleiades* or *Seven stars*. *Alcyone*, the central star of the group, being, it is said, on the same meridian as the pyramid, when it was constructed, and *Alpha* of Draconis, the then pole star, at its lower culmination.

But if, as the Rev. Joseph A. Seiss and others pretend, the scientific attainments required for the construction of such enduring monument surpassed those of the learned men of Egypt, we must, of necessity, believe that the architect who conceived the plan and carried out its designs must have acquired his knowledge from an older people, possessing greater learning than the priests of Memphis; unless we try to persuade ourselves, as the reverend gentleman wishes us to, that the great pyramid was built under the direct inspiration of the Almighty.

Nearly all the monuments of Yucatan bear evidence that the Mayas had a predilection for number SEVEN. Since we find that their artificial mounds were composed of seven superposed platforms; that the city of Uxmal contained seven of these mounds; that the north side of the palace of King CAN was adorned with seven turrets; that the entwined serpents, his totem, which adorn the east façade of the west wing of this building, have seven rattles; that the head-dress of kings and queens were adorned with seven blue feathers; in a word, that the number SEVEN prevails in all places and in everything where Maya influence has predominated.

It is a FACT, and one that may not be altogether devoid of significance, that this number SEVEN seems to have been the mystic number of many of the nations of antiquity. It has even reached our times as such, being used as symbol by several of the secret societies existing among us.

If we look back through the vista of ages to the dawn of civilized life in the countries known as the *old world*, we find this number SEVEN among the Asiatic nations as well as in Egypt and Mayab. Effectively, in Babylon, the celebrated temple of *the seven lights* was made of *seven* stages or platforms. In the hierarchy of Mazdeism, the *seven marouts*, or genii of the winds, the *seven amschaspands;* then among the Aryans and their descendants, the *seven horses* that drew the chariot of the sun, the *seven apris* or shape of the flame, the *seven rays* of Agni, the *seven manons* or criators of the Vedas; among the Hebrews, the *seven days* of the creation, the *seven lamps* of the ark and of Zacharias's vision, the *seven branches* of the golden candlestick, the *seven days* of the feast of the dedication of the temple of Solomon, the *seven years* of plenty, the *seven years* of famine; in the Christian dispensation, the *seven* churches with the *seven* angels at their head, the *seven* golden candlesticks, the *seven seals* of the book, the *seven* trumpets of the angels, the *seven heads* of the beast that rose from the sea, the *seven vials* full of the wrath of God, the *seven* last plagues of the Apocalypse; in the Greek mythology, the *seven* heads of the hydra, killed by Hercules, etc.

The origin of the prevalence of that number SEVEN amongst all the nations of earth, even the most remote from each other, has never been satisfactorily explained, each separate people giving it a different interpretation, according to their belief and to the tenets of their religious creeds. As far as the Mayas are concerned, I think to have found that it originated with the *seven* members of CAN's family, who were the founders of the principal cities of *Mayab*, and to each of whom was dedicated a mound in Uxmal and a turret in their palace. Their names, according to the inscriptions carved on the monuments raised by them at Uxmal and Chichen, were— CAN (serpent) and ooz (bat), his wife, from whom were born CAY (fish), the pontiff; AAK (turtle), who became the governor of Uxmal; CHAACMOL (leopard), the warrior, who became the husband of his sister Moó (macaw), the Queen of *Chichen*, worshiped after her death at Izamal; and NICTÉ (flower), the priestess who, under the name of *Zuhuy-Kuk*, became the goddess of the maidens.

The Egyptians, in expressing their ideas in writing, used three different kinds of characters—phonetic, ideographic and symbolic—placed either in vertical columns or in horizontal lines, to be read from right to left, from left to right, as indicated by the position of the figures of men or animals. So, also, the Mayas in their writings employed phonetic, symbolic and ideographic signs, combining these often, forming monograms as we do to-day, placing them in such a manner as best suited the arrangement of the ornamentation of the façade of the edifices. At present we can only speak with certainty of the monumental inscriptions, the books that fell in the hands of the ecclesiastics at the time of the conquest having been destroyed. No truly genuine written monuments of the Mayas are known to exist, except those inclosed within the sealed apartments, where the priests and learned men of MAYAB hid them from the *Nahualt* or *Toltec* invaders.

As the Egyptians, they wrote in vertical columns and horizontal lines, to be read generally from right to left. The space of this small essay does not allow me to enter in more details; they belong naturally to a work of different nature. Let it therefore suffice, for the present purpose, to state that the comparative study of the language of the Mayas led us to suspect that, as it contains words belonging to nearly all the known languages of antiquity, and with exactly the same meaning, in their mode of writing might be found letters or characters or signs used in those tongues. Studying with attention the photographs made by us of the inscriptions of Uxmal and Chichen, we were not long in discovering that our surmises were indeed correct. The inscriptions, written in squares or parallelograms, that might well have served as models for the ancient hieratic Chaldeans, of the time of King Uruck, seem to contain ancient Chaldee, Egyptian and Etruscan characters, together with others that seem to be purely Mayab.

Applying these known characters to the decipherment of the inscriptions, giving them their accepted value, we soon found that the language in which they are written is, in the main, the vernacular of the aborigines of Yucatan and other parts of Central America to-day. Of course, the original mother tongue having suffered some alterations, in consequence of changes in customs induced by time, invasions, intercourse with other nations, and the many other natural causes that are known to affect man's speech.

The Mayas and the Egyptians had many signs and characters identical; possessing the same alphabetical and symbolical value in both nations. Among the symbolical, I may cite a few: *water, country or region, king, Lord, offerings, splendor,* the *various emblems of the sun* and many others. Among the alphabetical, a very large number of the so-called Demotic, by Egyptologists, are found even in the inscription of the *Akabɔib* at Chichen; and not a few of the most ancient Egyptian hieroglyphs in the mural inscriptions at Uxmal. In these I have been able to discover the Egyptian characters corresponding to our own.

A a, B, C, CH or K, D, T, I, L, M, N, H, P, TZ, PP, U, OO, X, having the same sound and value as in the Spanish language, with the exception of the K, TZ, PP and X, which are pronounced in a way peculiar to the Mayas. The inscriptions also contain these letters, A, I, X and PP identical to the corresponding in the Etruscan alphabet. The finding of the value of these characters has enabled me to decipher, among other things, the names of the founders of the city of UXMAL; as that of the city itself. This is written apparently in two different ways: whilst, in fact, the sculptors have simply made use of two homophone signs, notwithstanding dissimilar, of the letter M. As to the name of the founders, not only are they written in alphabetical characters, but also in ideographic, since they are accompanied in many instances by the totems of the personages: e. g for AAK, which means turtle, is the image of a turtle; for CAY (fish), the image of a fish; for Chaacmol (leopard) the image of a leopard; and so on, precluding the possibility of misinterpretation.

Having found that the language of the inscriptions was

Maya, of course I had no difficulty in giving to each letter its proper phonetic value, since, as I have already said, Maya is still the vernacular of the people.

I consider that the few facts brought together will suffice at present to show, if nothing else, a strange similarity in the workings of the mind in these two nations. But if these remarkable coincidences are not merely freaks of hazard, we will be compelled to admit that one people must have learned it from the other. Then will naturally arise the questions, Which the teacher? Which the pupil? The answer will not only solve an ethnological problem, but decide the question of priority.

I will now briefly refer to the myth of Osiris, the son of *Seb and Nut*, the brother of *Aroeris*, the elder *Horus*, of *Typho*, of *Isis*, and of *Nephthis*, named also NIKÉ. The authors have given numerous explanations, result of fancy; of the mythological history of that god, famous throughout Egypt. They made him a personification of the inundations of the NILE; ISIS, his wife and sister, that of the irrigated portion of the land of Egypt; their sister, *Nephthis*, that of the barren edge of the desert occasionally fertilized by the waters of the Nile; his brother and murderer *Tipho*, that of the sea which swallows up the *Nile*.

Leaving aside the mythical lores, with which the priests of all times and all countries cajole the credulity of ignorant and superstitious people, we find that among the traditions of the past, treasured in the mysterious recesses of the temples, is a history of the life of Osiris on Earth. Many wise men of our days have looked upon it as fabulous. I am not ready to say whether it is or it is not; but this I can assert, that, in many parts, it tallies marvelously with that of the culture hero of the Mayas.

It will be said, no doubt, that this remarkable similarity is a mere coincidence. But how are we to dispose of so many coincidences? What conclusion, if any, are we to draw from this concourse of so many strange similes?

In this case, I cannot do better than to quote, verbatim, from Sir Gardner Wilkinson's work, chap. xiii :

> "*Osiris*, having become King of Egypt, applied himself towards civilizing "his countrymen, by turning them from their former barbarous course of "life, teaching them, moreover, to cultivate and improve the fruits of the "earth. * * * * With the same good disposition, he afterwards "traveled over the rest of the world, inducing the people everywhere to "submit to his discipline, by the mildest persuasion."

The rest of the story relates to the manner of his killing by his brother Typho, the disposal of his remains, the search instituted by his wife to recover the body, how it was stolen again from her by *Typho*, who cut him to pieces, scattering them over the earth, of the final defeat of Typho by Osiris's son, Horus.

Reading the description, above quoted, of the endeavors of Osiris to civilize the world, who would not imagine to be perusing the traditions of the deeds of the culture heroes *Kukulcan* and Quetzalcoatl of the Mayas and of the Aztecs? Osiris was particularly worshiped at Philo, where the history of his life is curiously illustrated in the sculptures of a small retired chamber, lying nearly over the western adytum of the temple, just as that of Chaacmol in the mural paintings of his funeral chamber, the bas-reliefs of what once was his mausoleum, in those of the queen's chamber and of her box in the tennis court at Chichen.

> "The mysteries of Osiris were divided into the greater and less mysteries. "Before admission into the former, it was necessary that the initiated "should have passed through all the gradations of the latter. But to merit "this great honor, much was expected of the candidate, and many even of "the priesthood were unable to obtain it. Besides the proofs of a virtuous "life, other recommendations were required, and to be admitted to all the "grades of the higher mysteries was the greatest honor to which any one "could aspire. It was from these that the mysteries of Eleusis were bor- "rowed." Wilkinson, chap. xiii.

In Mayab there also existed mysteries, as proved by symbols discovered in the month of June last by myself in the monument generally called the *Dwarf's House*, at Uxmal. It seemed that the initiated had to pass through different gradations to reach the highest or third; if we are to judge by the number of rooms dedicated to their performance, and the disposition of said rooms. The strangest part, perhaps, of this discovery is the information it gives us that certain signs and symbols were used by the affiliated, that are perfectly identical to those used among the masons in their symbolical lodges. I have lately published in *Harper's Weekly*, a full description of the building, with plans of the same, and drawings of the signs and symbols existing in it. These secret societies exist still among the *Zuñis* and other Pueblo Indians of New Mexico, according to the relations of Mr. Frank H. Cushing, a gentleman sent by the Smithsonian Institution to investigate their customs and history. In order to comply with the mission intrusted to him, Mr. Cushing has caused his adoption in the tribe of the Zuñis, whose language he has learned, whose habits he has adopted. Among the other remarkable things he has discovered is "the existence of twelve "sacred orders, with their priests and their secret rites as "carefully guarded as the secrets of freemasonry, an "institution to which these orders have a strange resem- "blance." (From the New York *Times*.)

If from Egypt we pass to Nubia, we find that the peculiar battle ax of the Mayas was also used by the warriors of that country; whilst many of the customs of the inhabitants of equatorial Africa, as described by Mr. DuChaillu in the relation of his voyage to the "Land of Ashango," so closely resemble those of the aborigines of Yucatan as to suggest that intimate relations must have existed, in very remote ages, between their ancestors; if the admixture of African blood, clearly discernible still, among the natives of certain districts of the peninsula, did not place that *fact* without the peradventure of a doubt. We also see figures in the mural paintings, at Chichen, with strongly marked African features.

We learned by the discovery of the statue of Chaacmol, and that of the priestess found by me at the foot of the altar in front of the shrine of *Ix-cuina*, the Maya Venus, situated at the south end of *Isla Mugeres*, it was customary with persons of high rank to file their teeth in sharp points like a saw. We read in the chronicles that this fashion still prevailed after the Spanish conquest; and then by little and little fell into disuse. Travelers tells us that it is yet in vogue among many of the tribes in the interior of South America; particularly those whose names seem to connect with the ancient Caribs or Carians.

Du Chaillu asserts that the Ashangos, those of Otamo, the Apossos, the Fans, and many other tribes of equatorial Africa, consider it a mark of beauty to file their front teeth in a sharp point. He presents the Fans as confirmed cannibals. We are told, and the bas-reliefs on Chaacmol's mausoleum prove it, that the Mayas devoured the hearts of their fallen enemies. It is said that, on certain grand occasions, after offering the hearts of their victims to the idols, they abandoned the bodies to the people, who feasted upon them. But it must be noticed that these last-mentioned customs seemed to have been introduced in the country by the Nahualts and Aztecs; since, as yet, we have found nothing in the mural paintings to cause us to believe that the Mayas indulged in such barbaric repasts, beyond the eating of their enemies' hearts.

The Mayas were, and their descendants are still, confirmed believers in witchcraft. In December, last year, being at the hacienda of X-Kanchacan, where are situated the ruins of the ancient city of Mayapan, a sick man was brought to me. He came most reluctantly, stating that he knew what was the matter with him: that he was doomed to die unless the spell was removed. He was emaciated, seemed to suffer from malarial fever, then prevalent in the place, and from the presence of tapeworm. I told him I could restore him to health if he would heed my advice. The fellow stared at me for some time, trying to find out, probably, if I was a stronger wizard than the *H-Men* who had bewitched him. He must have failed to discover on my face the proverbial distinctive marks great sorcerers are said to possess; for, with an incredulous grin, stretching his thin lips tighter over his teeth, he simply replied: "No use—I am bewitched—there is no remedy for me."

Mr. Du Chaillu, speaking of the superstitions of the inhabitants of Equatorial Africa, says: "The greatest "curse of the whole country is the belief in sorcery or "witchcraft. If the African is once possessed with the "belief that he is bewitched his whole nature seems to "change. He becomes suspicious of his dearest friends. "He fancies himself sick, and really often becomes sick "through his fears. At least seventy-five per cent. of "the deaths in all the tribes are murders for supposed "sorcery." In that they differ from the natives of Yucatan, who respect wizards because of their supposed supernatural powers.

From the most remote antiquity, as we learn from the writings of the chroniclers, in all sacred ceremonies the Mayas used to make copious libations with *Balché*. Today the aborigines still use it in the celebrations of their ancient rites. *Balché* is a liquor made from the bark of a tree called Balché, soaked in water, mixed with honey and left to ferment. It is their beverage *par excellence*. The nectar drank by the God of Greek Mythology.

Du Chaillu, speaking of the recovery to health of the King of *Mayo*lo, a city in which he resided for some time, says: "Next day he was so much elated with the "improvement in his health that he got tipsy on a fer-"mented beverage which he had prepared two days be-"fore he had fallen ill, and which he made by *mixing* "*honey and water, and adding to it pieces of bark of* "*a certain tree.*" (Journey to Ashango Land, page 183.)

I will remark here that, by a strange *coincidence*, we not only find that the inhabitants of Equatorial Africa have customs identical with the MAYAS, but that the name of one of their cities MAYO*lo*, seems to be a corruption of MAYAB.

The Africans make offerings upon the graves of their departed friends, where they deposit furniture, dress and food—and sometimes slay slaves, men and women, over the graves of kings and chieftains, with the belief that their spirits join that of him in whose honor they have been sacrificed.

I have already said that it was customary with the Mayas to place in the tombs part of the riches of the deceased and the implements of his trade or profession; and that the great quantity of blood found scattered round the slab on which the statue of Chaacmol is reclining would tend to suggest that slaves were sacrificed at his funeral.

The Mayas of old were wont to abandon the house where a person had died. Many still observe that same custom when they can afford to do so; for they believe that the spirit of the departed hovers round it.

The Africans also abandon their houses, remove even the site of their villages when death frequently occur; for, say they, the place is no longer good; and they fear the spirits of those recently deceased.

Among the musical instruments used by the Mayas there were two kinds of drums—the *Tunkul* and the *Zacatan*. They are still used by the aborigines in their religious festivals and dances.

The *Tunkul* is a cylinder hollowed from the trunk of a tree, so as to leave it about one inch in thickness all round. It is generally about four feet in length. On one side two slits are cut, so as to leave between them a strip of about four inches in width, to within six inches from the ends; this strip is divided in the middle, across, so as to form, as it were, tongues. It is by striking on those tongues with two balls of india-rubber, attached to the end of sticks, that the instrument is played. The volume of sound produced is so great that it can be heard, is is said, at a distance of six miles in calm weather. The *Zacatan* is another sort of drum, also hollowed from the trunk of a tree. This is opened at both ends. On one end a piece of skin is tightly stretched. It is by beating on the skin with the hand, the instrument being supported between the legs of the drummer, in a slanting position, that it is played.

Du Chaillu, Stanley and other travelers in Africa tell us that, in case of danger and to call the clans together, the big war drum is beaten, and is heard many miles around. Du Chaillu asserts having seen one of these *Ngoma*, formed of a hollow log, nine feet long, at Apono; and describes a *Fan* drum which corresponds to the *Zacatan* of the Mayas as follows: "The cylinder was about "four feet long and ten inches in diameter at one end, but "only seven at the other. The wood was hollowed out "quite thin, and the skin stretched over tightly. To beat "it the drummer held it slantingly between his legs, and "with two sticks beats furiously upon the upper, which "was the larger end of the cylinder."

We have the counterpart of the fetish houses, containing the skulls of the ancestors and some idol or other, seen by Du Chaillu, in African towns, in the small huts constructed at the entrance of all the villages in Yucatan. These huts or shrines contain invariably a crucifix; at times the image of some saint, often a skull. The last probably to cause the wayfarer to remember he has to die; and that, as he cannot carry with him his worldly treasures on the other side of the grave, he had better deposit some in the alms box firmly fastened at the foot of the cross. Cogolludo informs us these little shrines were anciently dedicated to the god of lovers, of histrions, of dancers, and an infinity of small idols that were placed at the entrance of the villages, roads and staircases of the temples and other parts.

Even the breed of African dogs seems to be the same as that of the native dogs of Yucatan. Were I to describe these I could not make use of more appropriate words than the following of Du Chaillu: "The pure bred na-"tive dog is small, has long straight ears, long muzzle "and long curly tail; the hair is short and the color yel-

"lowish; the pure breed being known by the clearness of "his color. They are always lean, and are kept very "short of food by their owners. * * * Although "they have quick ears; I don't think highly of their "scent. They are good watch dogs."

I could continue this list of similes, but methinks those already mentioned as sufficient for the present purpose. I will therefore close it by mentioning this strange belief that Du Chaillu asserts exists among the African warriors: *"The charmed leopard's skin worn about the warrior's middle is supposed to render that worthy spear-proof."*

Let us now take a brief retrospective glance at the FACTS mentioned in the foregoing pages. They seem to teach us that, in ages so remote as to be well nigh lost in the abyss of the past, the *Mayas* were a great and powerful nation, whose people had reached a high degree of civilization. That it is impossible for us to form a correct idea of their attainments, since only the most enduring monuments, built by them, have reached us, resisting the disintegrating action of time and atmosphere. That, as the English of to-day, they had colonies all over the earth; for we find their name, their traditions, their customs and their language scattered in many distant countries, among whose inhabitants they apparently exercised considerable civilizing influence, since they gave names to their gods, to their tribes, to their cities.

We cannot doubt that the colonists carried with them the old traditions of the mother country, and the history of the founders of their nationality; since we find them in the countries where they seem to have established large settlements soon after leaving the land of their birth. In course of time these traditions have become disfigured, wrapped, as it were, in myths, creations of fanciful and untutored imaginations, as in Hindostan: or devises of crafty priests, striving to hide the truth from the ignorant mass of the people, fostering their superstitions, in order to preserve unbounded and undisputed sway over them, as in Egypt.

In Hindostan, for example, we find the Maya custom of carrying the children astride on the hips of the nurses. That of recording the vow of the devotees, or of imploring the blessings of deity by the imprint of the hand, dipped in red liquid, stamped on the walls of the shrines and palaces. The worship of the mastodon, still extant in India, Siam, Burmah, as in the worship of *Ganeza*, the god of knowledge, with an elephant head, degenerated in that of the elephant itself.

Still extant we find likewise the innate propensity of the Mayas to exclude all foreigners from their country; even to put to death those who enter their territories (as do, even to-day, those of Santa Cruz and the inhabitants of the Tierra de Guerra) as the emissaries of Rama were informed by the friend of the owner of the country, the widow of the *great architect*, MAYA, whose name HEMA means in the Maya language "she who places ropes across the roads to impede the passage." Even the history of the death of her husband MAYA, killed with a thunderbolt, by the god *Pourandara*, whose jealousy was aroused by his love for her and their marriage, recalls that of *Chaacmol*, the husband of *Moó*, killed by their brother Aac, by being stabbed by him three times in the back with a spear, through jealousy—for he also loved *Moó*.

Some Maya tribes, after a time, probably left their home at the South of Hindostan and emigrated to Afghanistan, where their descendants still live and have villages on the North banks of the river *Kabul*. They left behind old traditions, that they may have considered as mere fantasies of their poets, and other customs of their forefathers. Yet we know so little about the ancient Afghans, or the Maya tribes living among them, that it is impossible at present to say how much, if any, they have preserved of the traditions of their race. All we know for a certainty is that many of the names of their villages and tribes are pure American-Maya words: that their types are very similar to the features of the bearded men carved on the pillars of the castle, and on the walls of other edifices at Chichen-Itza: while their warlike habits recall those of the Mayas, who fought so bravely and tenaciously the Spanish invaders.

Some of the Maya tribes, traveling towards the west and northwest, reached probably the shores of Ethiopia; while others, entering the Persian Gulf, landed near the embouchure of the Euphrates, and founded their primitive capital at a short distance from it. They called it *Hur* (*Hula*) *city of guests just arrived*—and according to Berosus gave themselves the name of *Khaldi;* probably because they intrenched their city: *Kal* meaning intrenchment in the American-Maya language. We have seen that the names of all the principal deities of the primitive Chaldeans had a natural etymology in that tongue. Such strange coincidences cannot be said to be altogether accidental. Particularly when we consider that their learned men were designated as MAGI, (Mayas) and their Chief *Rab-Mag*, meaning, in Maya, the *old man;* and were great architects, mathematicians and astronomers. As again we know of them but imperfectly, we cannot tell what traditions they had preserved of the birthplace of their forefathers. But by the inscriptions on the tablets or bricks, found at Mugheir and Warka, we know for a certainty that, in the archaic writings, they formed their characters of straight lines of uniform thickness; and inclosed their sentences in squares or parallelograms, as did the founders of the ruined cities of Yucatan. And from the signet cylinder of King Urukh, that their mode of dressing was identical with that of many personages represented in the mural paintings at Chichen-Itza.

We have traced the MAYAS again on the shores of Asia Minor, where the CARIANS at last established themselves, after having spread terror among the populations bordering on the Mediterranean. Their origin is unknown: but their customs were so similar to those of the inhabitants of Yucatan at the time even of the Spanish conquest— and their names CAR, *Carib* or *Carians*, so extensively spread over the western continent, that we might well surmise, that, navigators as they were, they came from those parts of the world; particularly when we are told by the Greek poets and historians, that the goddess MAIA was the daughter of *Atlantis.* We have seen that the names of the khati, those of their cities, that of Tyre, and finally that of Egypt, have their etymology in the Maya.

Considering the numerous coincidences already pointed out, and many more I could bring forth, between the attainments and customs of the Mayas and the Egyptians; in view also of the fact that the priests and learned men of Egypt constantly pointed toward the WEST as the birthplace of their ancestors, it would seem as if a colony, starting from Mayab, had emigrated Eastward, and settled on the banks of the Nile; just as the Chinese to-day, quitting their native land and traveling toward the rising sun, establish themselves in America.

In Egypt again, as in Hindostan, we find the history of the children of CAN, preserved among the secret traditions treasured up by the priests in the dark recesses of their temples: the same story, even with all its details. It is TYPHO who kills his brother OSIRIS, the husband of their sister ISIS. Some of the names only have been changed when the members of the royal family of CAN, the founder of the cities of Mayab, reaching apotheosis, were presented to the people as gods, to be worshiped.

That the story of *Isis* and *Osiris* is a mythical account of CHAACMOL and MOÓ, from all the circumstances connected with it, according to the relations of the priests of Egypt that tally so closely with what we learn in Chichen-Itza from the bas-reliefs, it seems impossible to doubt.

Effectively, *Osiris* and *Isis* are considered as king and queen of the Amenti—the region of the West—the mansion of the dead, of the ancestors. Whatever may be the etymology of the name of Osiris, it is a *fact,* that in the sculptures he is often represented with a spotted skin suspended near him, and Diodorus Siculus says: "That "the skin is usually represented without the head; but "some instances where this is introduced show it to be "the *leopard's* or *panther's.*" Again, the name of Osiris as king of the West, of the Amenti, is always written, in hieroglyphic characters, representing a crouching *leopard* with an eye above it. It is also well known that the priests of Osiris wore a *leopard* skin as their ceremonial dress.

Now, Chaacmol reigned with his sister Moó, at Chichen-Itza, in Mayab, in the land of the West for Egypt. The name *Chaacmol* means, in Maya, a *Spotted* tiger, a *leopard;* and he is represented as such in all his totems in the sculptures on the monuments; his shield being made of the skin of leopard, as seen in the mural paintings.

Osiris, in Egypt, is a myth. Chaacmol, in Mayab, a reality. A warrior whose mausoleum I have opened; whose weapons and ornaments of jade are in Mrs. Le Plongeon's possession; whose heart I have found, and sent a piece of it to be analysed by professor Thompson of Worcester, Mass.; whose effigy, with his name inscribed on the tablets occupying the place of the ears, forms now one of the most precious relics in the National Museum of Mexico.

Isis was the wife and sister of Osiris. As to the etymology of her name the Maya affords it in IƆIN—*the younger sister.* As Queen of the Amenti, of the West, she also is represented in hieroglyphs by the same characters as her husband—a *leopard, with an eye above,* and the sign of the feminine gender an oval or egg. But as a goddess she is always portrayed with wings; the vulture being dedicated to her; and, as it were, her totem.

Moó the wife and sister of *Chaacmol* was the Queen of Chichen. She is represented on the Mausoleum of Chaacmol as a *Macaw* (Moó in the Maya language); also on the monuments at Uxmal: and the chroniclers tell us that she was worshiped in Izamal under the name of *Kinich-Kakmó;* reading from right to left the *fiery macaw with eyes like the sun.*

Their protecting spirit is a *Serpent*, the totem of their father CAN. Another Egyptian divinity, *Apap* or *Apop*, is represented under the form of a gigantic serpent covered with wounds. Plutarch in his treatise, *De Iside et Osiride*, tells us that he was enemy to the sun.

TYPHO was the brother of Osiris and Isis; for jealousy, and to usurp the throne, he formed a conspiration and killed his brother. He is said to represent in the Egyptian mythology, the sea, by some; by others, *the sun*.

AAK (turtle) was also the brother of Chaacmol and Moó. For jealousy, and to usurp the throne, he killed his brother at treason with three thrusts of his *spear* in the back. Around the belt of his statue at Uxmal used to be seen hanging the heads of his brothers CAY and CHAACMOL, together with that of Moó ; whilst his feet rested on their flayed bodies. In the sculpture he is pictured surrounded by the *Sun* as his protecting spirit. The escutcheon of Uxmal shows that he called the place he governed the land of the Sun. In the bas-reliefs of the Queen's chamber at Chichen his followers are seen to render homage to the *Sun*; others, the friends of Moó, to the *Serpent*. So, in Mayab as in Egypt, the *Sun* and *Serpent* were inimical. In Egypt again this enmity was a myth, in Mayab a reality.

AROERIS was the brother of Osiris, Isis and Typho. His business seems to have been that of a peace-maker.

CAY was also the brother of *Chaacmol, Moó* and *Aac*. He was the high pontiff, and sided with Chaacmol and Moó in their troubles, as we learn from the mural paintings, from his head and flayed body serving as trophy to Aac as I have just said.

In June last, among the ruins of *Uxmal*, I discovered a magnificent bust of this personage; and I believe I know the place where his remains are concealed.

NEPHTHIS was the sister of Isis, Osiris, Typho, and Aroeris, and the wife of Typho; but being in love with Osiris she managed to be taken to his embraces, and she became pregnant. That intrigue having been discovered by Isis, she adopted the child that Nephthis, fearing the anger of her husband, had hidden, brought him up as her own under the name of Anubis. Nephthis was also called NIKÉ by some.

NIC or NICTÉ was the sister of *Chaacmol, Moó, Aac*, and *Cay*, with whose name I find always her name associated in the sculptures on the monuments. Here the analogy between these personages would seem to differ, still further study of the inscriptions may yet prove the Egyptian version to contain some truth. *Nic* or *Nicte* means flower; a cast of her face, with a flower sculptured on one cheek, exists among my collections.

We are told that three children were born to Isis and Osiris: Horus, Macedo, and Harpocrates. Well, in the scene painted on the walls of Chaacmol's funeral chamber, in which the body of this warrior is represented stretched on the ground, cut open under the ribs for the extraction of the heart and visceras, he is seen surrounded by his wife, his sister *Nic*, his mother *Zoo*, and four children.

I will close these similes by mentioning that *Thoth* was reputed the preceptor of Isis; and said to be the inventor of letters, of the art of reckoning, geometry, astronomy, and is represented in the hieroglyphs under the form of a baboon (cynocephalus). He is one of the most ancient divinities among the Egyptians. He had also the office of scribe in the lower regions, where he was engaged in noting down the actions of the dead, and presenting or reading them to Osiris. One of the modes of writing his name in hieroglyphs, transcribed in our common letters, reads *Nukta;* a word most appropriate and suggestive of his attributes, since, according to the Maya language, it would signify to understand, to perceive, *Nuctah:* while his name Thoth, maya *thot* means to scatter flowers; hence knowledge. In the temple of death at Uxmal, at the foot of the grand staircase that led to the sanctuary, at the top of which I found a sacrificial altar, there were six cynocephali in a sitting posture, as Thoth is represented by the Egyptians. They were placed three in a row each side of the stairs. Between them was a platform where a skeleton, in a kneeling posture, used to be. To-day the cynocephali have been removed. They are in one of the yard of the principal house at the Hacienda of Uxmal. The statue representing the kneeling skeleton lays, much defaced, where it stood when that ancient city was in its glory.

In the mural paintings at Chichen-Itza, we again find the baboon (Cynocephalus) warning Moó of impending danger. She is pictured in her home, which is situated in the midst of a garden, and over which is seen the royal insignia. A basket, painted blue, full of bright oranges, is symbolical of her domestic happiness. She is sitting at the door. Before her is an individual pictured physically deformed, to show the ugliness of his character and by the flatness of his skull, want of moral qualities, (the proving that the learned men of Mayab understood phrenology). He is in an persuasive attitude; for he has come to try to seduce her in the name of another. She rejects his offer: and, with her extended hand, protects the armadillo, on whose shell the high priest read her destiny when yet a child. In a tree, just above the head of the man, is an ape. His hand is open and outstretched, both in a warning and threatening position. A serpent (*can*), her protecting spirit, is seen at a short distance coiled, ready to spring in her defense. Near by is another serpent, entwined round the trunk of a tree. He has wounded about the head another animal, that, with its mouth open, its tongue protruding, looks at its enemy over its shoulder. Blood is seen oozing from its tongue and face. This picture forcibly recalls to the mind the myth of the garden of Eden. For here we have the garden, the fruit, the woman, the tempter.

As to the charmed *leopard* skin worn by the African warriors to render them invulnerable to spears, it would seem as if the manner in which Chaacmol met his death, by being stabbed with a spear, had been known to their ancestors; and that they, in their superstitious fancies, had imagined that by wearing his totem, it would save them from being wounded with the same kind of weapon used in killing him. Let us not laugh at such a singular conceit among uncivilized tribes, for it still prevails in Europe. On many of the French and German soldiers, killed during the last German war, were found talismans composed of strips of paper, parchment or cloth, on which were written supposed cabalistic words or the name of some saint, that the wearer firmly believed to be possessed of the power of making him invulnerable.

I am acquainted with many people—and not ignorant—who believe that by wearing on their persons rosaries, made in Jerusalem and blessed by the Pope, they enjoy immunity from thunderbolts, plagues, epidemics and other misfortunes to which human flesh is heir.

That the Mayas were a race autochthon on this western continent and did not receive their civilization from Asia or Africa, seems a rational conclusion, to be deduced from the foregoing FACTS. If we had nothing but their *name* to prove it, it should be sufficient, since its etymology is only to be found in the American Maya language.

They cannot be said to have been natives of Hindostan, since we are told that, in very remote ages, *Maya*, a prince of the Davanas, established himself there. We do not find the etymology of his name in any book where mention is made of it. We are merely told that he was a wise magician, a great architect, a learned astronomer, a powerful Asoura (demon), thirsting for battles and bloodshed: or, according to the Sanscrit, a Goddess, the mother of all beings that exist—gods and men.

Very little is known of the Mayas of Afghanistan, except that they call themselves *Mayas*, and that the names of their tribes and cities are words belonging to the American Maya language.

Who can give the etymology of the name *Magi*, the learned men amongst the Chaldees. We only know that its meaning is the same as *Maya* in Hindostan: magician, astronomer, learned man. If we come to Greece, where we find again the name *Maia*, it is mentioned as that of a goddess, as in Hindostan, the mother of the gods: only we are told that she was the daughter of Atlantis—born of Atlantis. But if we come to the lands beyond the waters of the Atlantic Ocean, then we find a country called MAYAB, on account of the porosity of its soil; that, as a sieve (*Mayab*), absorbs the water in an incredibly short time. Its inhabitants took its name from that of the country, and called themselves *Mayas*. It is a fact worthy of notice, that in their hieroglyphic writings the sign employed by the Egyptians to signify a *Lord*, a *Master*, was the image of a sieve. Would not this seem to indicate that the western invaders who subdued the primitive inhabitants of the valley of the Nile, and became the lords and masters of the land, were people from MAYAB; particularly if we consider that the usual character used to write the name of Egypt was the sieve, together with the sign of land?

We know that the *Mayas* deified and paid divine honors to their eminent men and women after their death. This worship of their heroes they undoubtedly carried, with other customs, to the countries where they emigrated; and, in due course of time, established it among their inhabitants, who came to forget that MAYAB was a locality, converted it into a personalty: and as some of their gods came from it, Maya was considered as the *Mother of the Gods*, as we see in Hindostan and Greece.

It would seem probable that the Mayas did not receive their civilization from the inhabitants of the Asiatic peninsulas, for the religious lores and customs they have in common are too few to justify this assertion. They would simply tend to prove that relations had existed between them at some epoch or other; and had interchanged some of their habits and beliefs as it happens, between the civilized nations of our days. This appears to be the true side of the question; for in the figures sculptured on the obelisks of Copan the Asiatic type is plainly discernible; whilst the features of the statues that adorn the celebrated temples of Hindostan are, beyond all doubts, American.

The FACTS gathered from the monuments do not sustain the theory advanced by many, that the inhabitants of tropical America received their civilization from Egypt and Asia Minor. On the contrary. It is true that I have shown that many of the customs and attainments of the Egyptians were identical to those of the Mayas; but these had many religious rites and habits unknown to the Egyptians; who, as we know, always pointed towards the West as the birthplaces of their ancestors, and worshiped as gods and goddesses personages who had lived, and whose remains are still in MAYAB. Besides, the monuments themselves prove the respective antiquity of the two nations.

According to the best authorities the most ancient monuments raised by the Egyptians do not date further back than about 2,500 years B. C. Well, in Aké, a city about twenty-five miles from Merida, there exists still a monument sustaining thirty-six columns of *katuns*. Each of these columns indicate a lapse of one hundred and sixty years in the life of the nation. They then would show that 5,760 years has intervened between the time when the first stone was placed on the east corner of the uppermost of the three immense superposed platforms that compose the structure, and the placing of the last capping stone on the top of the thirty-sixth column. How long did that event occur before the Spanish conquest it is impossible to surmise. Supposing, however, it did take place at that time; this would give us a lapse of at least 6,100 years since, among the rejoicings of the people this sacred monument being finished, the first stone that was to serve as record of the age of the nation, was laid by the high priest, where we see it to-day. I will remark that the name AKÉ is one of the Egyptians' divinities, the third person of the triad of Esneh; always represented as a child, holding his finger to his mouth. AKÉ also means a *reed*. To-day the meaning of the word is lost in Yucatan.

Cogolludo, in his history of Yucatan, speaking of the manner in which they computed time, says:

"They counted their ages and eras, which they in-
" scribed in their books every twenty years, in lustrums
" of four years. * * * When five of these lustrums
" were completed, they called the lapse of twenty years
" *katun*, which means to place a stone down upon an-
" other. * * * In certain sacred buildings and in
" the houses of the priests every twenty years they
" place a hewn stone upon those already there. When
" seven of these stones have thus been piled one over the
" other began the *Ahau katun*. Then after the first lus-
" trum of four years they placed a small stone on the
" top of the big one, commencing at the east corner; then
" after four years more they placed another small stone
" on the west corner; then the next at the north; and
" the fourth at the south. At the end of the twenty
" years they put a big stone on the top of the small ones:
" and the column, thus finished, indicated a lapse of one
" hundred and sixty years."

There are other methods for determining the approximate age of the monuments of Mayab:

1st. By means of their actual orientation; starting from the *fact* that their builders always placed either the faces or angles of the edifices fronting the cardinal points.

2d. By determining the epoch when the mastodon became extinct. For, since *Can* or his ancestors adopted the head of that animal as symbol of deity, it is evident they must have known it; hence, must have been contemporary with it.

3d. By determining when, through some great cataclysm, the lands became separated, and all communications between the inhabitants of *Mayab* and their colonies were consequently interrupted. If we are to credit what Psenophis and Sonchis, priests of Heliopolis and Saïs, said to Solon "that nine thousand years before, the visit to them of the Athenian legislator, in consequence of great earthquakes and inundations, the lands of the West disappeared in one day and a fatal night," then we may be able to form an idea of the antiquity of the ruined cities of America and their builders.

Reader, I have brought before you, without comments, some of the FACTS, that after ten years of research, the paintings on the walls of *Chaacmol's* funeral chamber, the sculptured inscriptions carved on the stones of the crumbling monuments of Yucatan, and a comparative study of the vernacular of the aborigines of that country, have revealed to us. I have no theory to offer. Many years of further patient investigations, the full interpretation of the monumental inscriptions, and, above all, the possession of the libraries of the learned men of *Mayab*, are the *sine qua non* to form an uncontrovertible one, free from the speculations which invalidate all books published on the subject heretofore.

If by reading these pages you have learned something new, your time has not been lost ; nor mine in writing them.

www.ingramcontent.com/pod-product-compliance
Lightning Source LLC
Chambersburg PA
CBHW031605110426
42742CB00037B/1265